Schooling and Education in Lebanon

Nina Maadad & Grant Rodwell

Schooling and Education in Lebanon

Syrian and Syrian Palestinian Refugees Inside and Outside the Camps

PETER LANG
Bern · Berlin · Bruxelles · Frankfurt am Main · New York · Oxford · Wien

Bibliographic information published by die Deutsche Nationalbibliothek
Die Deutsche Nationalbibliothek lists this publication in the Deutsche Nationalbibliografie; detailed bibliographic data is available on the Internet at ‹http://dnb.d-nb.de›.

British Library Cataloguing-in-Publication Data: A catalogue record for this book is available from The British Library, Great Britain.

Library of Congress Control Number: 2016960138

Political map of Lebanon, Map No. 4282, January 2010, United Nations (http://www.un.org/Depts/Cartographic/map/profile/lebanon.pdf) – copyright permission granted by
Ms. Ayako Kagawa
Geographic Information Officer (GIO)
Chief Cartographic Unit
Geospatial Information Section (formerly Cartographic Section)
Division for Information and Telecommunications Technologies (ICTD)
Department of Field Support (DFS)
United Nations

ISBN 978-3-0343-2381-9 pb.
ISBN 978-3-0343-2382-6 eBook
ISBN 978-3-0343-2384-0 MOBI
ISBN 978-3-0343-2383-3 EPUB

Wabernstrasse 40, CH-3007 Bern, Switzerland
info@peterlang.com, www.peterlang.com

Contents

Dedication

The authors would like to dedicate this book to all those displaced children, their parents and teachers in scattered refugee camps throughout the world.

Our responsibility and duty as parents and carers is to provide the best education for our children, love and protect them, but also to give them the freedom and stability that allows them to have a normal childhood and to dream of their future, a future they create for themselves so they can live their lives as we did before them. Nothing says it better than the renowned words of wisdom recorded by the famous Lebanese poet and writer Gibran Khalil Gibran in his book, *The Prophet*:

> Your children are not your children. They are the sons and daughters of life's longing for itself. They come through you but not from you, and though they are with you yet they belong not to you … (Gibran Khalil Gibran, 1923).

Acknowledgements

We would like to express our deepest appreciation to all those who helped us and made it possible for us to gather information for this book. Visiting schools, homes and camps during such difficult times in Lebanon would have been impossible to achieve without the help and support of school principals, teachers, parents, students and stakeholders who sacrificed their time to provide us with information and made sure that we were safe. We would also like to thank family and friends for accompanying us on our visits, ensuring our safety and introducing us to people and places. A specific thank you also to the family members who carried out some extra interviews on our behalf since our departure from Lebanon on late matters and provided us with feedback. Last, but not least, a huge thank you to Dr Marizon Yu for her great work on the diagram and the cross-referencing to it, as well as her tireless support.

Nina especially wishes to thank the University of Adelaide for providing her with study leave and financial support to travel to Lebanon in the second part of 2014. Without this opportunity it would have been impossible to meet the large number of humble and generous people including family, friends, children, parents, teachers, principals and community leaders interviewees; which allowed us to gather the information needed to complete this book.

We are most grateful to everyone involved in this journey, and acknowledge the fact that we could have not completed this book without their help.

Acronymns and Abbreviations

ALP	Accelerated Learning Programs
AVSI	Association of Volunteers in International Services
CERD	Centre of Education Research and Development
CRC	Convention on the Rights of the Child
EFA	Education for All
IGO	International Governmental Organization
INGO	International Non-Governmental Organization
INEE	International network for Education in Emergencies
MoEHE	Ministry of Education and Higher Education
MOE	Syrian Ministry of Education
NFE	Non-formal education
NGO	Non-Governmental Organization
PRS	Palestinian Refugees from Syria
RACE	Reaching All Children with Education
UN	United Nations
UNHCR	United Nations High Commission for Refugees
UNICEF	United Nations International Childrens Emergency Fund
UNRWA	United Nations Refugee Works Agency
WILPF	Women's International League for Peace and Freedom

Preface

Most people viewing the state funeral of former Australian Prime Minister Malcolm Fraser on 27th March 2015 at Scots' Church in Melbourne's CBD would have been most impressed by a large group of Vietnamese Australians present, complete with a large sign proclaiming their thanks to a man who, as Prime Minister from 1975 to 1983, welcomed them to Australian shores, and through government policy, facilitated their Australian citizenship. As his son, Hugh Fraser, emphatically stated in his eulogy, Fraser was a "truly global man", who loved Australia, and who in his public and private life really cared for what was happening globally, to the extent he could not remain silent in the face of such events as global refugees (*News.com.au*, 2015, n.p.).

News.com.au (2015) also reported:

> The volume of public mourners spread across the corner of Russell and Collins streets to St Michael's Uniting Church where screens telecast the service and police shut down traffic.
>
> Australia's Vietnamese community were among those to turn out to farewell Mr Fraser.
>
> General secretary of the Vietnamese community in Victoria Phong Nguyen said it was like losing their own parent.
>
> "We call him our father and our saviour," Mr Nguyen said on Friday.
>
> "He means everything to us but mostly freedom for saving us from the refugee camp. It's a very deep loss for our community" (n.p.)

In the dark shadow of the Australian government's present immigration policy and its lack of general support for the world's refugees, the authors of this book take great inspiration from these scenes and words at Malcolm Fraser's funeral, and long for the day when all Australians can be thus eulogised and described. Fraser was an inspiration for all.

The initial encouragement for this book came during a time in Australia's history when asylum seekers to our shores experienced a particularly difficult time because of the Australian Coalition government's policy of Operation Sovereign Borders. Set against these terrible circumstances was the inglorious civil war in Syria, rendering terrible destruction on millions of Syrian families, especially disrupting the schooling of millions of children.

A Lebanese Australian, working as an academic in the School of Education, University of Adelaide, as a part of her study leave taken in Semester 2 of 2014, Nina Maadad, travelled to Lebanon during the second part of 2014, to undertake the fieldwork.

In understanding Nina's motivation to travel to her home country of Lebanon to investigate Syrian refugee children and schooling, we need to understand she was motivated by such fellow Lebanese Australians as Joseph Wakim (2013) who has argued that Australians have much to learn from Lebanon in respect to refugees. Wakim (2013) has contended "tiny Lebanon, with its population of just over four million, has accommodated around one million refugees from the war in Syria. By contrast, only about one in 600 residents in Australia are asylum seekers or refugees. Our policy makers need to adopt a global perspective". Wakim (2013) went on to stress how Australians need to develop a global perspective in this regard:

> Prime Minister Kevin Rudd's recent attempt to focus these two lenses of the Australian binoculars on boat people was missing the third lens: a global perspective.
>
> When asked if we could be "more compassionate to the refugees" at a community cabinet meeting in Rockhampton, Rudd should have known that compassion requires a lens from the outside looking in, not the reverse.
>
> On the other side of the world where I was born, my four million Lebanese compatriots have accommodated over one million Syrian refugees, and counting. Ironically, even the 500,000 Palestinians in south Lebanon refugee camps have opened their tents to the Syrian families (n.p.).

Inspired by such people as Wakim and Malcolm Fraser, this book is a contribution to that global perspective.

Introduction

The goal of this book is to provide insights into the education and schooling of children inside and outside Lebanese refugee camps. What is happening to children and young refugees in terms of their schooling? What experiences and challenges do these refugee children and young people have? This book aims to investigate the perspectives of children, their parents, teachers, community leaders, and state politicians and bureaucrats on the schooling provisions and educational opportunities for refugee children in Lebanon.

It must be emphasised that the refugees come from various socio-economic and cultural groups, mostly from Syria and the rest from Palestine and Iraq (UNHCR, 2013). These refugee camps are scattered all over Lebanon. The United Nations High Commissioner for Refugees (UNHCR), in partnership with the relevant Lebanese Government ministries, runs these camps. A total of four camps – two Syrian and two Syrian Palestinian – are represented in the data and a total of eight schools are included. In total, the forty-eight respondents represent the sample clusters of children, parents, teachers, community leaders and state officials. It must be clarified that even though refugee camps in Lebanon also embraced Palestians and Iraqis who fled their conflict-riddled countries, this book is limited to refugees that fled Syria during the armed conflict of 2011, and these include Syrians and Palestinian refugees from Syria (PRS).

While in Lebanon, Nina visited the country's Syrian and Palestinian-Syrian refugee camps and refugees in other communities in Lebanon, seeking responses from a variety of stakeholders on provisions for formal schooling, and education generally: children, parents, teachers, community leaders, and views from state authorities.

Nina was determined to gather first-hand knowledge on how Syrian refugee children and young adults responded to their severely changed circumstances in a new country. She wanted to meet with these people and gain some understanding of how the students or would-be-students regarded formal school education following the noticeable mass dislocation in their lives. Would these young people look to renew their schooling in their new camp environment, or would they avoid formal schooling and conform to some stereotypical views of students' views of school avoidance? Moreover, if formal schooling was made available what would conditions be like – the curriculum, support material, buildings and so on? What are students' views of this new school environment?

Nina recognised caring for their children's housing and health needs would always be a high priority for refugee parents, but if these were secured, how would they prioritise their children's formal schooling? What provisions would their host country, Lebanon, provide? Under the stress of these changed circumstances and in the possible absence of state provisions, would parents respond in some cooperative manner and organise formal schooling for their children? What other responses from parents would manifest themselves?

Teaching can be a stressful occupation at any time, anywhere in the world, but how do teachers respond to these conditions in Syrian refugee camps and villages and towns where presumably conditions are much more stressed? How do they respond to the needs of the refugee children and young adults? What level of support do teachers receive from parents, the community and the state? How do teachers perceive their role in the camp and neighbouring schools? Nina anticipated interviewing teachers with these and many other questions.

Most people recognise formal schooling has an ameliorating effect on chaotic communities. Presumably, most leaders in the Syrian refugee camps and in surrounding Lebanese communities would recognise how schooling can have an enormously positive effect on communities, and would respond positively to the needs of the Syrian refugees. How did they view these new arrivals – particularly in their own country, which only a few decades earlier had been terribly ravaged by its own civil war? For many decades there have been tens of thousands of Palestinian refugees in Lebanon. Specifically, what measure, if any, would they put in place to assist the new arrivals?

Before returning to her home country, Nina was aware state authorities were restricted in a number of ways they could support the schooling of Syrian refugee children. For decades they had been making provisions for the Palestinian refugees. To what level could international authorities – the UNHCR and so on – respond to the chaos of these camps in respect to the schooling needs of the refugee children and young adults?

It was a moving experience for Nina as she visited the country of her birth, witnessing the chaos caused by the neighbouring Syrian war madness. She departed, however, with a wonderful and elevated sense of belief in her fellow human beings.

There are millions of stories – a million tragedies, most in the form of the country's children. Next to their health needs, parents look to formal education to ameliorate their children's life chances – not necessarily education in a general sense, but formal school education with certificates at the end of it in order they might use them to progress through life. Parents recognise the value of formal schooling in almost every instance. It is one thing to be educated, for example to have achieved a certain standard in mathematics, but in the refugee environment it is another thing to have earned a piece of paper – to possess a piece of paper, a certificate from a recognised education authority to testify to having achieved that required standard. That certificate of educational achievement becomes a necessity to an individual's life chances – something for which most parents strive. But what happens when there are no schools available? Amazingly, in most cases, the human spirit knows no bounds.

It was not surprising that Nina was quickly able to meet individuals who were prepared to come together and establish schools, in many cases with volunteer teachers. This is collective action to which young people respond when they see their parents and elders striving to this end. Enthusiasm is contagious.

Generally, this book is addressed to all people concerned with the plight of the children and their attempts to provide formal education for Syrian people who are living in Lebanon's refugee camps and other centres and areas. Particularly, however, it is addressed to students and teachers, and undergraduates in universities. From the authors' anecdotal experiences, despite the large numbers of overseas students in Australian universities, there is an inadequate level of discourse in universities concerning what actually happens in the Syrian refugee camps in Lebanon. Often global perspectives can be quite limited.

It is our desire that the international values such as those possessed by Malcolm Fraser, and almost universally acclaimed, may be renewed in the current and future generations of Australia's young people. We hope for another Malcolm Fraser, or potential Malcolm Fraser, on every seat in every Australian university lecture theatre.

An international tragedy: The tragedy of the displaced

The conflict in Syria has now been raging for four years – since the early northern spring of 2011 – and as a result of this tragedy, over one and a half million Syrian refugees have looked for shelter in Lebanon alone. Of these 630,000 are between the ages three to eighteen (Shuayb, 2014). It should be pointed out that we are not including those who fled to Jordan, Turkey and Iraq to seek shelter (Shuayb, Makkouk & Tuttunji, 2014). In 2015 we have already reached the number of registered refugees that was originally projected for 2050 (Shaheen, 2014b). There are many contributing factors to the overwhelming number of refugees settling in Lebanon. The two main reasons are: first, the open borders between Syria and Lebanon while other countries restricted crossings; and secondly, the fact that many Syrians have lived in Lebanon since the 1950s and already established families and political or business ties (Thibos, 2014). These factors have made Lebanon very accessible for many Syrian families fleeing the conflict.

The president of WILPF, Nouha Ghosn, posted online on 8th October 2013 the fact that a large number of Syrians arriving in Lebanon did not register, an action necessary for their own protection and security. This is because of their political beliefs concerning the Assad regime in their home country (Ghosn, 2013). Refugees are primarily scattered in areas in the north, the Bekaa, the middle areas of Mount Lebanon and the south-west region extending from Beirut to Saida and Sour near the Israeli border.

The map below highlights the areas where the Syrian refugees are living.

It has been estimated that 155,000 people (15%) out of the refugee population live in tented settlements because the Lebanese government originally refused to build a formal refugee camp. Understandably, this tragic situation has put the Lebanese local communities under great strain in terms of being able to provide employment, healthcare, housing, hygiene, living costs and of course education (Thibos, 2014).

For many, it is inconceivable Syrian refugees had to run away and leave behind everything they once owned, worked and lived for, homes, family members, friends, possessions. It is also even crueller and frightening to imagine in such situations what children tend to go through and how they end up paying the highest price. Children tend to face dangers every minute of their lives, lose loved ones, watch family members being killed and get killed themselves, become orphans or are even mutilated. In short, the children lose their childhood, they lose the meaning of a beautiful world they would like to live in, and they lose the sense of innocence and the excitement and joy of being alive. Our focus in this book is mainly on schooling and its availability to the Syrian refugee children in the camps and in other communities in Lebanon.

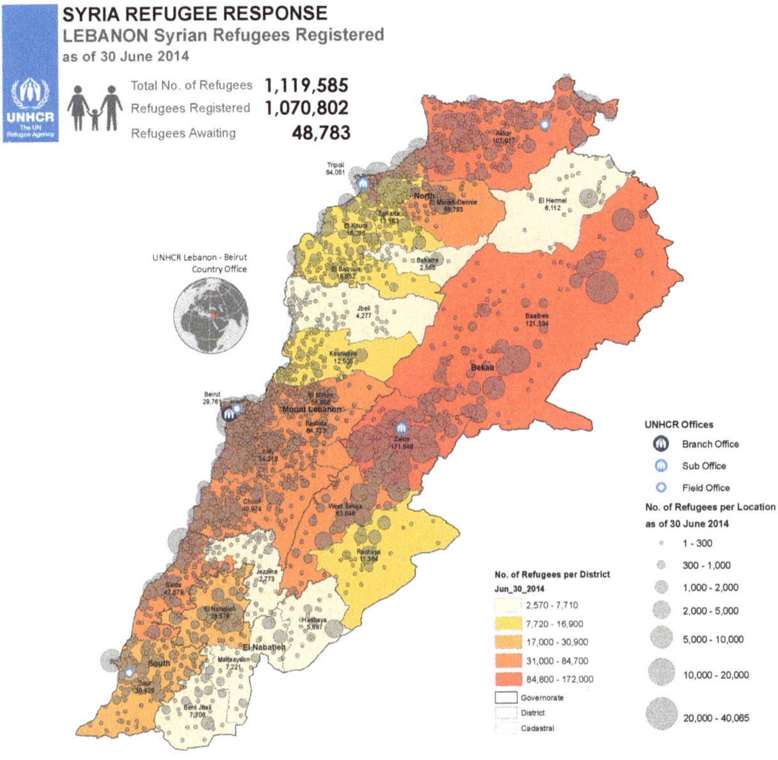

Figure 1: Concentration of Syrian Refugees in Lebanon (June 2014), source UNHCR, cited on 14 July 2015.

It has been estimated that thirty per cent of Lebanese children attend public schools out of a total population of approximately 900,000 school-age children. At the same time the Lebanese Ministry of Education and Higher Education (MoEHE) is currently struggling to accommodate the large number of refugee children due to both space/vacancy and budget pressures. Consequently private welfare organisations and NGOs have been requested to give support and funding for infrastructure. A recent study conducted by UNHCR (2014a) reveals that there are certain regulations in Lebanon limiting education rights to Lebanese citizens only, yet this is contradicted by international agreements such as the Convention on the Rights of the Child (CRC) and United Nations (UN) policies. These state that governments are obligated to provide schooling for all children under the age of fifteen.

References

Ghosn, N. (2013). Lebanon's burden: The crushing consequences of Syria's refugee crisis. *Women's International League for Peace and Freedom.* Retrieved 20 December 2014, from <www.wilpfinternational.org/Lebanons-burden-the-crushing-consequences-of-syrias-refugees--crisis/org.com>.

Shaheen, K. (2014b, 18 September). Four out of five Syrian children in Lebanon lack schooling. Retrieved 22 November 2014, from <http://www.dailystar.com.lb/News/Lebanon-News/2014/Sep-18/271039-four-out-of-five-syrian-children-in-lebanon-lack-schooling.ashx>.

Shuayb, M. (2014). A lost generation? Education opportunities for Syrian children in Lebanon. Retrieved 12 September 2014, from <http://www.rsc.ox.ac.uk/events/a-lost-generation-education-opportunities-for-syrian-refugee-children-in-lebanon>.

Shuayb, M., Makkouk, N. & Tuttunji, S. (2014). Widening access to quality education for Syrian refugees: The role of private and NGO sectors in Lebanon. Retrieved 13 October 2014, from <http://www.alnap.org/resource/19984>.

Thibos, C. (2014). One million Syrians in Lebanon: A milestone quickly passed. Retrieved 5 November 2014, from <http://www.migrationpolicycentre.eu/>.

United Nations High Commissioner for Refugees (UNHCR). (2013b). Syria regional response plan. Geneva: UNHCR.

Chapter One
Geopolitics, Middle East Conflicts, Communities, Refugees and Children

Introduction

During the northern summer of 2015 many Australians were shocked by the sheer number of desperate people from North Africa taking dangerous journeys on leaky boats to Italy, with the associated thousands of drownings. Meanwhile in Australia the Abbott Government claimed it "had stopped the boats" for asylum seekers to Australia's north, thus preventing these people from reaching Australian shores. At the same time many Australians were shaken by the numbers of the desperate asylum seekers from North Africa to Europe, apparently in their tens of thousands. Moreover, additionally and often concurrently, the media presented graphic stories of conflicts in Iraq and Syria and the emergence of a military organisation seeking to call itself Islamic State (IS). Accompanying these stories were others poignantly describing massive refugee camps in Turkey, Jordan, Lebanon and in North Africa. Sections of Middle-East Islamic countries were in turmoil. What happens to the children as parents search for the safety of the refugee camps in neighbouring countries?

Before proceeding further, the principal research methodology used in the book is discussed below.

Methodology

This book utilised a qualitative methodology in the tradition of Grounded Theory (Corbin & Strauss, 1990; Glaser, 2001; Glaser & Strauss, 1967) to provide understanding on schooling of refugee children in and outside refugee camps in Lebanon. In this methodology, the data collection and the analysis are interconnected. Sampling proceeds from a theoretical basis not in terms of number of camps, schools, or individuals, thus avoiding positivistic analysis of the data. Data collection was primarily undertaken through in-depth and open-ended interviews with knowledgeable respondents such as children and their parents in refugee camps and in schools, teachers, community leaders and government bureaucrats. Based on Glaserian Grounded Theory (Glaser, 2001), data analysis was undertaken in three stages: open coding, selective coding, and theoretical coding. With the first two stages, a process of constant comparative analysis allowed themes to emerge; these themes were grouped in categories as necessary. Emerging themes from the data included authentic cases of concepts such as social disadvantage, social conditions, schooling conditions, personal challenges, educational challenges, opportunities, coping strategies, trauma, resilience, and enabling structures. Concepts served as interpretive devices for the theoretical coding stage leading to the creation of substantive theories on the schooling of refugee children towards the discourse of the "pedagody of the displaced", which this book propositions. "Pedagogy of the displaced" is an offshoot of Freire's "pedagogy of the oppressed".

While theoretical knowledge cannot be disregarded in this book and literature on theoretical ideas contributes to rigour of analysis, adopting a grounded theory approach allows for the discovery of theory from the data. The qualitative analysis undertaken in the book is from "ground up" without being blind to existing theoretical frames and body of knowledge that can explain the situation and struggles of refugees. This book draws upon conflict theories to address the limitations of grounded theory. Thus, the methodological approach utilised in this book may be referred to as informed grounded theory (Thornberg, 2012).

The Arab Spring

The Arab Spring was a revolutionary wave of demonstrations and protests – both non-violent and violent – riots, and civil wars in the Arab world beginning on 18 December 2010 with the Tunisian Revolution, and spreading throughout the countries of the Arab League and its surroundings. While the wave of initial revolutions and protests faded by mid-2012, some started to refer to the succeeding and still ongoing large-scale discourse conflicts in the Middle East and North Africa as the "Arab Winter". The most radical discourse from Arab Spring into the still ongoing civil wars taking place in Syria and Iraq as early as the second half of 2011, continued unabated into at least 2016.

While it all began in Tunisia, by the end of February 2012, however, ruling elites had been forced from power there, from Egypt, from Libya and from Yemen. The media piled on graphic accounts to Westerners. Particularly alarming were the reports of tens of thousands of Muslims assembling in places such as Cairo's Tahrir Square and in other Egyptian cities such as Alexandria. Almost concurrently, there were other civil uprisings in Bahrain and Syria. Major protests had also broken out in Algeria, Iraq – already devastated by an Allied invasion – Jordan, Kuwait, Morocco and Sudan. Minor protests also occurred in Mauritania, Oman, Saudi Arabia, Djibouti, Western Sahara, and Palestine. Adding to this turbulence were Tuareg fighters and their weapons returning from the Libyan Civil War and stoking a simmering conflict in Mali which could be attributed to fallout from the Arab Spring in North Africa.

Constant media coverage was a feature of these conflicts. The protests also shared some techniques of civil resistance in sustained campaigns involving strikes, demonstrations, marches and rallies. The obvious and effective use of social media, often linked with mainstream media, used to organize, communicate, and raise awareness in the face of authoritarian attempts at repression and internet censorship were evident during these tumultuous times.

Westerners witnessed how in return, however, many Arab Spring demonstrations were being met with violent responses from authorities, as well as from pro-government militias and counter-demonstrators. These attacks were answered with violence from protestors in some cases. Australians were presented on the media with graphic accounts of how with another regime change in Egypt, three Al-Jazeera journalists, including Australia's Peter Greste and Canada's Mohamed Fahmy, were goaled simply for reporting news of the recently disposed Muslim Brotherhood. Graphic TV detail portrayed an Egyptian legal system working frantically in the interests of the ruling elites.

To begin with, many Western observers may have been hopeful about these post-colonial events, perhaps even anticipating similar post-Soviet upheavals that swept across Europe with the revolutions of 1989. Sadly, however, this was just the beginning of social upheavals which would precipitate mass movements of people in the Arab world. How are these events to be understood?

Social conflict theory

Social conflict theory is a Marxist-based sociological theory arguing that individuals and groups – or social classes – within society have differing amounts of material and non-material resources – such as access to education, and the fruits of educational attainment – and that the more powerful groups use their power in order to exploit groups with less power. Consider those families who seek an education for their children. The conflict theorist argues that this relationship is unequal and in emerging economies favours certain social groups and their political elites. The same applies to children from lower social economic groups for whom the state may provide an education, but it is of a type which ensured it is of a sufficiently low standard that will lock them into the social groups to which they were born. Here, as in numerous other examples, many children from labouring classes build a high sense of injustice when they seek an education, perhaps perceived as unobtainable. It is this type of relationship which conflict theorists use to illustrate that social relationships are about power and exploitation (Miller, 1986).

The conflict perspective, or conflict theory, derives from the ideas of Karl Marx, who postulated society as a dynamic entity constantly undergoing change driven by class conflict, and socio-economic class the basis of which is determined by modes of production. This theory can be juxtaposed to functionalism which postulates society as a complex system striving for equilibrium, whereas the conflict perspective views social life as competition. It is, however, an often associated deterministic aspect of social conflict theory which the authors of this book eschew, arguing for the free will of individuals, and the innate potential for individual betterment. This book is about refugees seeking education as a means of escape from their present condition. This is an act of free will.

According to the conflict perspective, society is made up of individuals competing for limited resources – for example, money, leisure, access to educational resources. Moreover, competition over scarce resources is at the heart of all social relationships. Social conflict theory postulates competition, rather than consensus, is characteristic of human relationships. Broader social structures and organizations – religions, government, educational institutions – reflect the competition for resources and the inherent inequality competition entails. Social conflict theory, especially perceives some people and organizations have more resources – power and influence – and use those resources to maintain their positions of power in society. Access to education is at the heart of these imperatives.

C. Wright Mills was a founder of modern conflict theory. He argued social structures are created because of conflict between differing interests. Social structures thus created, then impact on individuals and the usual result is a differential of power between the "elite" and the "others". Examples of elites are government and large corporations, and the school education systems developed in their interests (Mills, 1963). Sociologists who work from the conflict perspective, study the distribution of resources, power, and inequality, particularly the political underpinnings of power. Typically, they are concerned with social change and who benefits from social change. Social conflict theorists are drawn to mass social phenomena such as the Arab Spring and its repercussions such as mass migration of people as refugees.

While the competing sociological theory of functionalism emphasizes stability, conflict theory emphasizes change. According to the conflict perspective, society is constantly in conflict over resources, and that conflict drives social change. For example, conflict theorists might explain the Arab Spring and its repercussions by studying how activists challenged the unequal distribution of political power and economic resources in the immediate post-colonialist societies of the Middle East – for example, Egypt and Syria. As in these cases, conflict theorists generally see social change as abrupt, even revolutionary, as indeed, was so much that occurred in the Arab Spring. In the conflict perspective, change comes about through conflict between competing interests, not consensus or adaptation, or through incremental and negotiated measures. Conflict theory, therefore, gives sociologists a framework for explaining social change, thereby addressing one of the perceived problems with the functionalist perspective, that of Whiggish or triumphalist interpretations.

Predictably, conflict theory has been criticized for its focus on change and neglect of social stability, especially as postulated by functionalist sociologists. Some critics acknowledge societies are in a constant state of change, but point out that much of the change is minor or incremental, not revolutionary. For example, many modern capitalist states have avoided revolutions, and have instead instituted elaborate social service programs, as was the case with Australia's history. Although conflict theorists often focus on social change, they have, in fact, also developed a theory to explain social stability (Miller, 1986). According to the conflict perspective, inequalities in power and reward are built into all social structures. Individuals and groups who benefit from any particular structure strive to see it maintained. For example, the wealthy and powerful elites may fight to maintain their privileged access to such institutions as higher education by opposing measures that would broaden access, such as affirmative action or public funding. This explains much of the drive for school education in Lebanon's refugee camps visited by Nina Maadad as described in the subsequent chapters of this book.

Sectarianism and ethno-religious conflicts in the Middle East: state building and state-society relations

If there is one single defining characteristic of Islamic State it is its drive to be recognised as a state. This is counterbalanced by a drive by Western national leaders who refuse to do so. For example, the Australian Abbott Government refers to it as "the death cult". What is the significance of sectarianism in the on-going ethno-religious conflicts in the Middle East?

Matthieson (2014) notes the significance of sectarianism as a salient feature of politics and society for the last ten years in the Middle East and elsewhere. Moreover, for Matthieson (2014, p. 1):

> The prominence of religious conflict is astonishing on several levels: first of all, it contradicts secularisation and modernisation theories … The rise of sectarianism is in part related to the resurgence of religion and new religious movements across the globe.

Particularly, for Matthieson (2014, p. 1), in a post-colonial world this:

> Forces us to reconsider the nature of state building and state-society relations in the Middle East. States that were in the past seen as "strong", "nationalist" and governed by officially secular regimes, such as Iraq, Syria and Egypt, fractured along ethnic and sectarian lines. Others [such as the United Arab Emirates] are under constant challenge, or have seen an upsurge in sectarian violence and polemics.

Broadly speaking, in the Middle East there is a division between urban centres, where states established their capitals and power bases – largely dominated by Sunni Islam with its acceptance of unjust rulers often seen to be better than anarchy – and peripheral regions, where various sects managed to establish themselves and institutionalise communal systems of social, moral and at times political control. Iraq is a strong example of this. It is a country where Sunni and Shia Islam are often in sharp and hostile conflict, but, which prior to the Iraq War was controlled by the brutality of the Hussein regime.

Shia Islamists came to power in Iran in 1979 through their own making, and *vis-a-vis* strong resistance by the West, particularly the US. In Iraq, it was the US-led intervention that brought Shia Islamist parties to power, but indeed, shattered their grip through other geopolitical forces, such as the Al-Qaeda attack on the United States on 11 September 2001.

Led by the United States, the invasion of Iraq began on 20 March 2003. Without declaring war and with the excuse of ridding the country of supposed weapons of mass destruction (WMDs), the invading forces launched a "shock and awe" surprise attack. Iraqi forces were quickly overwhelmed as the invading forces swept through the country. The invasion led to the collapse of the Ba'athist government. The country's leader Saddam Hussein, a Sunni, was captured in December 2003 and executed by a military court three years later. However, the power vacuum following Saddam's demise and the mismanagement of the occupation, led to widespread sectarian violence between Shias and Sunnis, as well as a lengthy insurgency against US and coalition forces. The US responded with a troop surge in 2007, identified as the counter-insurgency (COIN) strategy; the heavy American security presence and deals made between the occupying forces and Sunni militias reduced the level of violence. The US began withdrawing its troops in the winter of 2007–2008.

Matthieson (2014, p. 2) sounds a warning about making colonialist assumptions when analysing events such as the Iraq War:

> When making these broad overviews and generalisations, we need to be aware that we do not fall into the trap of Orientalism or imperial design. Until fairly recently, the view of the Middle East as a mosaic of religions and ethnicities, many of whom are eternally at war with each other, dominated much of the academic and political debate about "the Orient". At the same time, authoritarian rulers, and colonial powers (including the Ottomans), used the notion of perpetual conflict between Sunni and Shia to make the case for the need of an external arbiter, a power broker.

Indeed, many Arab dictators and kings continue to use these same tactics to justify their rule. Iraq, Syria and Egypt are examples of this.

Matthieson (2014, p. 2) also asks readers to consider the highly nuanced nature of sectarianism:

> And we should also not use "sectarianism" as a catchall explanation for very different kinds of processes. Quite often we hear that something is "sectarian" and it is assumed that we understand what it means, but we often do not, or understand different things.
>
> But not talking about cultural difference is a mistake as well. Throughout much of the Middle East and the Islamic world, talking about sectarianism was largely a taboo.
>
> Since the 20th century, a number of "sects" have attained political power, in parts because of help from Western countries.

There has been a tragic history of colonialist powers using sectarianism to consolidate their influence in the Middle East. Matthieson (2014) reminds readers to consider how "the French institutionalisation of sectarianism in the political systems of the Levant did much to ensure by and large politics would be organised through the socio-political structures of "sects" ' (p. 2). France helped bring about an Alawite state, lasting from 1920 to 1936. The French refined the processes of power politics based on sectarianism that would have long-lasting post-colonialist influences. For example, they recruited many Alawites and members of other minorities into special branches of the army, which ensured that after independence these minorities were in a powerful position (Matthieson, 2014).

Earlier, building on past imperial sectarianism, the British also developed imperial politics based on sectarianism, the processes and products of which would last much longer than their empire. For example, in Egypt Christians, Circassians, Jews and others were vital in business and politics under the Ottomans, Muhammad Ali, and then under the British and the monarchy. Then with the British Empire in ruins, the nationalist upsurge and Nasser's nationalisation policies largely pushed them out of the centres of power. Only the Copts remained a significant part of the Egyptian social fabric (Matthieson, 2014).

Contributing to the rise of sectarianism

The politicization of Shia Islam and the empowerment of the Shia in the last decades and the Iranian revolution has contributed to the mix of sectarianism and geo-politics in foreign and security policies, particularly in Saudi Arabia and Iran, but increasingly also in other states such as Iraq, Syria and Bahrain.

Thus, we should note how the institutional legacies of Ottoman, French and British imperial rule have left socio-political institutions in the Middle East. This also should be seen in the light of how the failure of secular ideologies and the rise of Islamism have paved the way for the rise of sectarian politics. Various state and non-state actors have used sectarian politics to bolster their support base, delegitimise their political opponents, and seek international alliances, in response to the Arab uprisings since 2011 (Matthieson, 2014).

The fact that two resource-rich countries – Saudi Arabia and Iran – see themselves as protectors of Sunni and Shia communities respectively, fuels this Sunni-Shia sectarianism and internationalises these initially localised conflicts. The Iranian revolution and the 2003 Iraq War led to a change in the status of non-Sunni Islamic sects, undermining the self-perception amongst Sunni elites that they were the "natural" rulers of the Middle East, a process resulting in Iraq War. In addition, supported by oil money and the US, the spread of Salafi-Wahhabism has provided the language and ideology for this new form of sectarian politics. In Matthieson's (2014, n.p.) words "any attempt to defuse tensions in the region and to stop the spread of sectarian hatred needs to take into account the historical genealogies and political economies of sectarianism, as well its international dimension."

Power politics defining "community"

Given what has been written above in this chapter concerning social conflict theory, how might power politics in respect to community, play out in the vast number of refugee camps across the Middle East?

The accepted thinking is that a community is a social unit of any size sharing common values. Although embodied, or face-to-face, communities are usually small, larger or more extended, sociologists study other communities such as a national community, international community and virtual community. Common binding factors such as intent, belief, resources, preferences, needs, risks, and a number of other conditions may be present and common, affecting the identity of the participants and their degree of cohesiveness. It is not difficult to see how school education might fit here.

Since the advent of the internet, the concept of community has become less geographical, with fewer limitations. People can now gather virtually in an online community and share common interests regardless of physical location. Prior to the internet, virtual communities – like social or academic organizations – were far more limited by the constraints of available communication and transportation technologies. Today, Australians and people in other Western countries witness in graphic detail how young people apparently are drawn through the internet to Islamic State. To what extent this is an example of young people searching for a community of interest has yet to be fully researched.

Bulley (2014) writes how refugee camps are managed increasingly through a liberal rationality of government, similar to that of many industrialized societies, with security mechanisms being used to optimize the life of particular refugee populations. This governmentality has encompassed programmes introduced by the United Nations High Commissioner for Refugees (UNHCR) and various non-governmental organizations (NGOs) to build and empower communities through the spatial technology of the camp. Advocates of social conflict theory, would argue that this is an attempt by host nations to safeguard and secure themselves against potential conflict. How might a drive towards the establishment of formal school education fit this paradigm? As we journey with Nina through Lebanon's refugee camps the reader shall see how children, parents and community members look to school education as a means to a secure future, while at the same time assisting in community building.

Bulley (2014) goes on to argue such attempts to "govern through community" have been too easily dismissed or ignored. His research therefore examines how such programmes work to produce, manage and conduct refugees through the use of a highly instrumentalized understanding of community in the spatial and statistical management of displaced people in camps. The drive towards school education by the refugees in the camps and other places illustrates the role instrumentalities, supported by the government, might play in this process of community building.

However, Bulley (2014) shows community is always both more and less than what is claimed to be, and therefore undermines attempts to use it as a governing tactic, by shifting shifting to a more ontological understanding of community as unavoidable coexistence, inspired by Jean-Luc Nancy (The European Graduate School, 2012). Fitting the social conflict paradigm, Bulley (2014) argues the scripting of something is missing here! and government through community in camps is continually exceeded, redirected and resisted. Bulley (2014) also shows ethnographies of specific camps in Africa and the Middle East illustrate how the necessary sociality of being, resists its own instrumentalization, viewing the camp as a spatial security technology. Such resistance does not necessarily lead to greater security, but it redirects our attention to how community is used to conduct the behaviour of refugees, while also producing counter-conducts offering greater agency, meaning and mobility to those displaced in camps. In this regard as she journeys through Syrian refugee camps and other places in Lebanon, Nina looked to discover how various stakeholders of formal school education in the camps and elsewhere might perceive education for their own ends.

Global Governance: refugee conventions, the rights of the child

Throughout this book there is constant reference to such international organisations as the United Nations High Commissioner for Refugees (UNHCR) and global governance instruments such as the Refugee Convention, the Convention on the Rights of the Child. An analysis of these entities is relevant to this chapter.

Barnett (2002) shows how the UNHCR was created in the postwar Cold War climate with staunch opposition from the Soviets. It has its roots in the Treaty of Westphalia in 1648, and emerged in the form of the post-World War I League of Nations, before it was formalised in its present form. In the twenty-first century it faces stern challenges. Still, the Cold War had an overwhelming influence on the norms and rules of the regime, and the UNHCR has since struggled to adapt to changing global circumstances, particularly so in the transnational world of the twenty-first century, with its global scale of refugees. Thus this issue of refugees becomes an increasingly pressing one. Barnett (2002) argues gender and race are critical distributional issues. Barnett (2002, p. 239) concludes:

> Forced to reconsider its definition and policies, the emerging regime must create and environment where the collective international authority of the UN body has meaningful influence on the autonomous implementation of individual government policy. In a world where the rigid constructions of the traditional international system are beginning to crumble, established approaches to refugee policy are becoming irrelevant as well. The regime that took root in 1648 no longer dictates, as customary concepts of global governance adapt to an uncertain environment of shifting politics and security.

This simple outcome to this is, as Nina discovered as she visited the refugees in camps and other places in Lebanon, that many would-be refugees are turned back at borders, only to face an uncertain future.

The United Nations Convention: Refugees and the Rights of the Child

As the Australian Government "turn-back-the-boats" policy bites, in Australia there is much discourse amongst journalists, politicians and the public-at-large concerning Australia's obligations to the Refugee Convention. For many Australians, this in turn helps to turn our thoughts to the Middle East refugees.

"The 1951 Convention relating to the Status of Refugees is the key legal document in defining who is a refugee, his or her rights and the legal obligations of states. The 1967 Protocol removed geographical and temporal restrictions from the Convention" (UNHCR, 2015b). Yet, as with the UNHCR in the twenty-first century, all of this is under challenge. Witness the manner in which for blatant political reasons with the excuse that "they are only economic refugees", nations are able to turn back asylum seekers, or refuse to accept them (Millbank, 2000). If this happens in Australia, it surely must happen in the Middle East. Again, this book turns to the revelations of Nina's journey as she visits refugees in the camps and other places in Lebanon.

The whole question of the United Nations Convention on the Rights of the Child (UNCRC) is brought into focus as Australians view asylum seekers, many of them children, behind the razor wire of the camps on Manus Island and Nauru, on their TV screens and evidence the Australian Government's so-called Pacific Solution, which many of them support. This is particularly so when accusations of alleged manifold exploitations are revealed through the media. Yet, the UNCRC has much to be praised for in its role in these revelations.

Indeed, as Reynaert, Bouverne-de-Bie, and Vandevelde (2009) argue children's rights have become a significant field of study during the past decades, largely due to the adoption of the UNCRC in 1989. For these authors, "today, scholarly work on children"s rights is almost inconceivable without considering the Convention as the bearer of the children's rights debate" (p. 518). The authors attempt to explore critically academic work on the UNCRC. By means of a discourse analysis of international literature, the article maps the academic discourse on children's rights. Three themes are identified that predominate and challenge the academic work on the UNCRC:

- autonomy and participation rights as the new norm in children's rights practice and policy,
- children's rights versus parental rights and
- the global children's rights industry.

That these three themes distinguish contemporary scholarly work on the UNCRC might not be a coincidence, as the authors analyse them from the process of "educationalization" that has characterized childhood in western societies since the nineteenth century. With formal school education and refugee children being the focus of this book, the perspective of educationalization – or absence there of – presents a timely reference for this present study.

Conclusion

The changing relationship between Islam and politics, the rise of Gulf states as financial and political actors, and the Iranian Revolution, and the rise of IS, have all contributed to the development of contemporary sectarianism, at the same time being a driving force behind conflicts contributing to the Middle East refugee crisis. The empowerment of Shia movements across the region has led to fears amongst the old Sunni elites, who in turn supported a sectarian backlash. Political sectarianism is distinctively modern, related to political economy and geo-politics, with similar functions and logics as ethnic nationalism and related to processes of post-modernity. Sectarianism is also a fundamentalist phenomenon, trying to ascribe fixed categories and identities where these are often in flux or even eroding, and becoming more fluid and hybrid, be it through massive socio-economic changes, political disruptions, new technologies, or changes in social control and public morality. Surely, the Middle East refugee camps must carry many of these issues.

Reflecting on social conflict theory, readers can well understand how it is in the interests of Western countries to somehow build communities in the many Syrian refugee camps and other places of refuge in Lebanon. This is apart from the distinct humanitarian motive for any humanitarian intervention. To this end, as Nina travelled through the refugee camps and other places she was concerned with discovering the views of various stakeholders of this massive refugee occasion in regard to the role that formal school education might play in community building, and other motives that might drive the stakeholders to continue their education in such dire circumstances.

References

Barnett, L. (2002). *Global governance the evolution of the international regime*. New York: Oxford University Press.

Bulley, D. (2014). Inside the tent: Community and government in refugee camps *Security Dialogue*.

Matthiesen, T. (2014). Key issues in religion and world affairs: Sectarianism in the Middle East. Retrieved 26 June 2015, from <http://www.bu.edu/cura/files/2013/ 10/Matthiesen.pdf>.

Millbank, A. (2000). *The problem with the 1951 Refugee Convention*. Canberra: Commonwealth of Australia Retrieved from <http://www.aph.gov.au/About_Parliament/Parliamentary_Departments/Parlia mentary_Library/pubs/rp/rp0001/01RP05>.

Miller, P. (1986). *Long division*. Adelaide: Wakefield Press.

Mills, C. W. (1963). *Power, politics and people*. New York: Galaxy.

Reynaert, D., Bouverne-de-Bie, M. & Vandevelde, S. (2009). A review of children's rights literature since the adoption of the United Nations Convention on the Rights of the Child. *Childhood, 16*(4), 518–534. doi: 10.1177/0907568209344270.

The European Graduate School. (2012). Biography: Jean-Luc Nancy. Retrieved 3 July 2015, from <http://www.egs.edu/faculty/jean-luc-nancy/biography/>.

United Nations High Commissioner for Refugees (UNHCR). (2015b). The 1951 Refugee Convention,. Retrieved 3 July 2015, from <http://www.unhcr.org/pages/49da0e466.html>.

Chapter Two
Refugees in Lebanon: The Context

Introduction

The plight of Syrian refugees is shared by many countries. This chapter focuses on the Lebanese context, the problems, and the scope of the study in relation to these issues. Everybody suffers. A literature review reveals how the sustained political and socio-economic crises have the potential to rob generations of young people of their education and therefore career prospects. The grim reality of violent and ongoing conflicts has been very evident in Lebanon for more than two decades, a country in which refugee camps have attracted the attention of humanitarian services to provide education strategies that serve as part of broader development and relief schemes.

The lives of refugees have been the focus of considerable public concern in recent years and their situation has profound implications for economic development and social policy. The current and spiralling out-of-control civil war in Syria is leading to more pressures on Lebanon's refugee camps; it emerges that here there is a particular schooling context prevailing in them. In fact, one recent report documented that nearly a million Syrian refugees living in temporary conditions in Lebanon are approaching catastrophe and in desperate need of additional aid. The nature of the support being provided in the form of housing, schools, teachers, and actual education system change is discussed here, as well as the implications for the provision of education to children and youth in such circumstances.

The rise of the Lebanese refugee camps

Throughout history, it has been evident that during civil wars or periods of inter-ethnic strife, the failure of governments to maintain social and economic stability, as well as law and order, leads to the collapse of public institutions, of which schooling is an integral part. Sustained political and socio-economic crises have the potential to rob generations of young people of their schooling and therefore career prospects. As has often been the case in the history of displaced persons, children and particularly girls are the first to suffer.

Undoubtedly, refugees "have been the focus of considerable public concern in recent years" (Taylor, 2004, p. 1) and their situation has profound implications for economic development and social policy (Drumm, Pittman, & Perry, 2004). A literature review in the mid-1980s highlighted the importance of developing and maintaining health education programs in refugee camps, revealing that little health education was undertaken in refugee camps and little consensus existed as to what health education was (Simmons, 1985).

This literature review examines the issues concerning the "rolling out" of schooling in Lebanese refugee camps, and with particular reference to the post-conflict society. The current, and spiralling out-of-control, civil war in Syria is leading to more pressures on Lebanon's refugee camps and other types of community settlement, and it emerges here that there is a particular educational context prevailing in the camps. In fact, one recent report documented that nearly a million Syrian refugees "living in temporary conditions in Lebanon are approaching catastrophe and in desperate need of additional aid" (Powell, 2014; see also ANERA, 2014). The nature of the support being provided in the form of housing, schools, teachers, and actual change in the education system is discussed here, as well as the implications for the provision of education to children and youth in such circumstances. The complexity of the Lebanese civil war already has been much discussed.

The unfolding crisis

By April 2013, the Syrian civil war had been raging for almost two years. The flood of refugees to neighbouring countries had assumed tsunami-like proportions, as the rest of the world reeled in disbelief. According to Batha (2013, n.p.) "more than a million refugees have fled Syria during two years of fighting. Most have gone to Jordan, Lebanon, Turkey and Iraq". Not since the end of World War II had there been such a flood of refugees. Sarah Whyte and Inga Ting (2014) reported in the *Sydney Morning Herald*:

> The number of refugees, asylum-seekers and internally displaced people worldwide has exceeded 50 million for the first time since World War II, a United Nations report shows. …
>
> Last year there were 51.2 million people displaced worldwide, 6 million more than in 2012. Worsening conflicts in Syria, the Central African Republic and South Sudan caused major new numbers of refugees, the report said.
>
> Australia's refugee resettlement program was ranked second in the world in 2013, behind only the US and marginally ahead of Canada. These three countries hosted 90 per cent of resettled refugees in 2013.
>
> But resettled refugees – those admitted through a UNHCR program – account for less than 4 per cent of recognised refugees (n.p.).

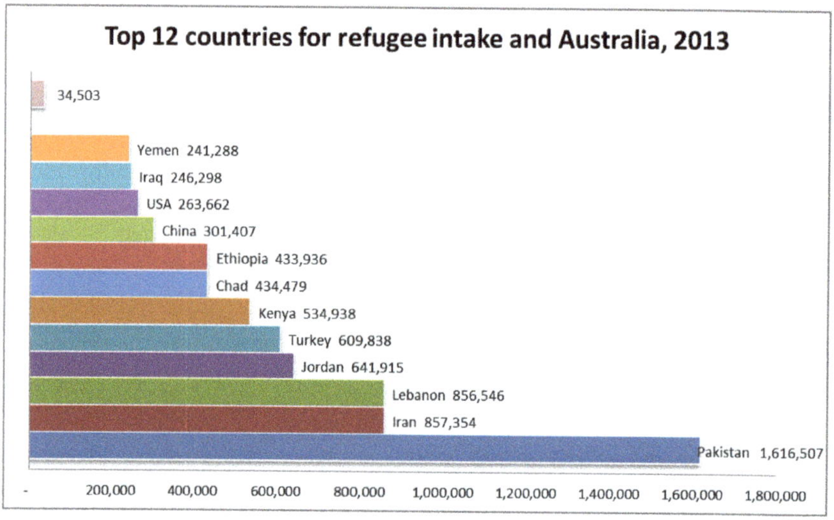

Figure 2: Refugee intake in 2013, top 12 countries including Australia, adapted from Whyte & Ting (2014).

New communities: home-sickness and community-building through schooling

Broadacre government housing development was a common feature of the Australian suburban scene from the 1960s to the 1980s, until the rise of the alternative concept of in-fill housing. During the mid-1970s Grant was an assistant principal at Rokeby Primary School on Hobart's Eastern Shore, one such broadacre government housing development in Tasmania. This was a time during the very early days of housing development. What was once hectares of pasture country suddenly became government housing, with sections given over to subsections, for example single-parent families – usually a mother and several children. As an assistant principal at the school, he had the responsibility to manage many of the behavioural issues, working closely with social workers, psychologists and counsellors.

Thinking back on my five years at Rokeby Primary School, and the abrupt transition of the landscape from bare pastures to government housing, where people came from all over the state to settle into a new suburb, I am inclined to think there were many similarities, albeit certainly not as austere, as the refugee camps of the Middle East. At the time, I was convinced that what we were doing in the school was more than just educating the children. Essentially, it was community building. Research by Bill Mulford *et al.* (2008) substantiates my intuitive judgment thirty years earlier. To what extent do schools and teachers contribute to community-building in Lebanese refugee camps?

There is a body of research showing schools not only educate and socialise students, but assist in building communities. We may extrapolate from here and state that schooling assists in linking the refugee community with host communities in many positive ways. When children are attending school regularly, the broader community becomes more settled and less prone to crime and other forms of anti-social behaviour (Gottfredson *et al.*, 2011; McCarthy *et al.*, 2003).

Writing in Dadaab, Kenya on behalf of the UNHCR, Duke Mwancha (2014) testifies to the ways in which schools are catalysts for community-building in refugee camps:

> Six years ago, Muuxi Adam met two friends in a coffee shop in the Canadian city of Winnipeg to talk about ways they could help other Somalis stuck in refugee camps in Africa.
>
> The three, all Somali but from different clans, started by setting up a non-governmental organization, Humankind International, to spread awareness about Somali refugees in neighbouring countries such as Kenya and Ethiopia, and to raise money for education projects for refugees.
>
> In February [2014], their initiative took concrete form with the opening of a preschool in the Dagahaley camp, part of the world's largest refugee camp complex at Dadaab in north-east Kenya. "More than 400 children lined up to enrol in the school, but we could only take 140 for now," Muuxi told UNHCR at the recent opening ceremony. He added that half were from the camp and half from the host community (n.p.).

Proximity to urban areas: health and education

Nina visited refugees in urban and rural settings, the latter which Lebanese refer to as mountains (as for the Matn) and valleys (as for the Bekaa). Urban-based refugees have attracted special attention from researchers. A UNHCR (2009) report showed:

> According to UNHCR's most recent statistics, almost half of the world's 10.5 million refugees now reside in cities and towns, compared to one third who live in camps.
>
> As well as increasing in size, the world's urban refugee population is also changing in composition. In the past, a significant proportion of the urban refugees registered with UNHCR in developing and middle-income countries were young men who possessed the capacity and determination needed to survive in the city.
>
> Today, however, large numbers of refugee women, children and older people are also to be found in urban areas, particularly in those countries where there are no camps. They are often confronted with a range of protection risks: the threat of arrest and detention, *refoulement*, harassment, exploitation, discrimination, inadequate and overcrowded shelter, as well as vulnerability to sexual and gender-based violence (SGBV), HIV-AIDS, human smuggling and trafficking (p. 2).

Indeed, Nina encountered vast numbers of refugee women and children with these concerns in her visits to the Lebanon refugee shelters researching how education and schooling might occur in these settings.

The proximity of refugee camps to urban areas is a significant factor in the refugees' quality of life. Thomas, Calvo and Loughry (2015) argue "refugees are increasingly migrating to urban areas, but little research has been conducted to compare health and wellbeing outcomes of urban refugees with those based in camps" (n.p.). The authors' analytic cross-sectional study investigated differences in health-related quality of life for urban and camp-based refugees in sub-Saharan Africa, and assessed the influences of both the environment and the perceived environment on refugees' health-related quality of life using the World Health Organization's Quality of Life scale (WHOQOL-BREF).

According to Thomas, Calvo and Loughry (2015), "refugees in urban environments reported significantly higher levels of satisfaction with overall health, physical health and environmental well being than refugees placed in camps" (n.p.). Based on the assumption that people learn better when they are well, education has an important role to play in these quality of life factors. A reading in the following chapters of Nina's visits to Syrian refugee camps in Lebanon shows this is also the case here. Why is this so?

Research by Thomas, Calvo and Loughry (2015) also showed "in multivariate analyses, urban environments were associated with better physical health for refugees, compared to camp environments" (n.p.). In addition, "refugees' perceptions of their environment, particularly feeling safe in daily life and in the home environment, as well as being satisfied with living conditions, were more strongly associated with physical health than the environment itself, whether urban or camp-based" (n.p.). Again, as exemplified by Nina's visit to Mr Fadel in Chapter Seven, health is everything when it comes to learning, especially in the challenges of refugee camps.

Of course, it is not just physical health which connects with a grounding for education and schooling. Mental health professionals also have researched the connection between mental health and effective schooling in refugee children. For example, Lustig, *et al.* (2004) sought to "to review stressful experiences and stress reactions among child and adolescent refugees" either in camps or resettlement programs "as well as interventions and ethical considerations in research and clinical work, within the framework of the chronological experiences of child refugees; namely, the phases of pre-flight, flight, and resettlement" (n.p.). Highlighted in this research were special refugee populations such as unaccompanied minors, asylum seekers, and former child soldiers. Pertinent medical findings were summarized.

The authors reviewed articles from 1990 to 2003 addressing the above issues, and found "child and adolescent refugees suffer from significant conflict-related exposures. Reactions to stress may be mediated by coping strategies, belief systems, and social relations" (n.p.). Lustig, *et al.* (2004) concluded "more research is needed on interventions, specifically on efficacy and cultural relevance. Interventions that have an impact on multiple ecological levels need further development and evaluation" (n.p.).

Further research by Porter and Haslam (2005) reinforced the findings of Lustig, *et al.* (2004) stated: "The global refugee crisis requires that researchers, policymakers, and clinicians comprehend the magnitude of the psychological consequences of forced displacement and the factors that moderate them. To date, no empirical synthesis of research on these issues has been undertaken" (n.p.). Moreover, "the sociopolitical context of the refugee experience is associated with refugee mental health. Humanitarian efforts that improve these conditions are likely to have positive impacts" (n.p.).

Early days in the refugee camps: "building" schools

In a report now over one decade old, UNHCR (2001) in its initial establishment of camps contends with the often "spurious arguments [advanced] against rapid educational response in refugee emergencies". Typically, these arguments are as follows:

- Education may prevent rapid voluntary repatriation;
- Staff are too busy, there are insufficient vehicles or staff housing;
- Education is not urgent, not life-saving (p. 24).

The UNHCR (2001) report goes on to remind us "refugees are normally homesick and their return from mass exile in neighbouring countries is delayed primarily by political and economic factors, and security issues. Decisions about repatriation are made by political leaders or tribal or family elders, [with] little concern over how young children spend their days" (p. 24). Despite these circumstances, however, the refugees establish their own schools – usually without buildings:

> The type of education that can take place in the first weeks of a refugee situation is very non-formal, with often unqualified teachers gathering children to play games, learn the alphabet, practice reading, writing and arithmetic, and so forth. It is unlikely to delay repatriation. Any items distributed are portable and can be taken back to the home country (p. 24).

Schools are not synonymous with physical school buildings. As the UNHCR (2001) puts it:

> Some people imagine that rapid education response means "building schools", but emergency education [schooling] frequently takes place under trees or plastic sheeting. School construction may happen later, in months or years (and by then, formal education would have started anyway). The argument that emergency education means "building schools" and will give a "feeling of permanence", is thus unrealistic (p. 24).

Clearly, it is the process of having students working with a teacher in a relatively planned and structured manner, complying with acceptable standards. This is schooling, taking its first tentative steps towards individual growth and community building.

Conflict-affected children: adjusting to the school environment

Teachers, who Nina and Grant know as having taught refugee children in Australian schools, affirm the difficulties faced when settling newly arrived refugee students into their classes and schools. Sidhu and Taylor (2012) support this observation, and through research in four case study Queensland schools, argue:

> The worldwide rise in numbers of refugees and asylum seekers suggests the need to examine the practices of those institutions charged with their resettlement in host countries. … Schooling … [plays a vital contribution] to the successful resettlement of refugee children. We begin with an examination of forced migration and its links with globalisation, and the barriers to inclusion confronting refugees. [There] is s

> discussion of the educational challenges confronting individual refugee youth and schools … and the approaches they had developed to meet the needs of young people from a refugee background. … [concluding] by discussing how educational institutions might play a more active role in facilitating transitions to citizenship for refugee youth through an inclusive approach (n.p.).

Clearly, adapting to a new school environment is one of the major tasks facing refugee children when they arrive in a new country or in the first place in a refugee camp. Anecdotal evidence from teachers in Australian schools accommodating refugee children suggests the existence of traumatised children. What is clear is that education, generally, and schooling in particular, are crucial in the psychosocial adjustment and cognitive growth of refugee children. It is through the school environment, with experienced and appropriately trained teachers, that these traumatised children are detected, providing opportunities for referral for further appropriate treatment. Due to these circumstances, it is important for educators to consider the needs, obstacles, and successful educational pathways for children refugees (Bridging Refugee Youth and Children's Services, 2006).

Indeed, Fazel and Stein (2002) show how, typically, children have experienced at least three stages of trauma:

> (1) In their native countries many refugees have experienced considerable trauma. They have often been forced to flee their homes because of exposure war or combat and hence witnessed violence, torture, and losses of close family and friends. Refugee children might have no memory of a period of stability; their school education, if any, is likely to have been disrupted; and parental distress and general insecurity are common experiences.
>
> (2) The journey to a country of refuge can also be a time of further stress. It can take many months and expose the refugees to more life threatening dangers. Refugee children at these times can experience separation from parents, either by accident or as a strategy to ensure their safety. As international immigration controls tighten, more children are being placed in the hands of smugglers to ensure their escape, either as the only representative their family can afford to send away or in the hope that the child alone would have better chances of gaining refugee status.
>
> (3) The final stage of finding respite in another country can be a time of additional difficulty as many have to prove their asylum claims and also try to integrate in a new society. This period is being increasingly referred to as a period of "secondary trauma" to highlight the problems encountered. On arriving, a refugee child will need to settle into a new school and find a peer group. Children might have to prematurely assume adult roles; for example, as a vital language link with the outside world (p. 366).

While Fazel and Stein (2002) researched and wrote their article from the point of view of refugees being resettled in the UK, one can imagine that this trauma could only be more accentuated in refugee camps in a foreign country. The researchers argue even though refugee students value education as an agent for change, they may not find success in school. In fact they may encounter other obstacles, such as:

- Disrupted schooling. Refugee children may experience disrupted schooling in their country of origin or an absence of schooling altogether. Teachers will agree that it is extremely difficult for a student with no previous education to enter into a classroom with educated children.
- The various stages of trauma referred to above.
- School dropouts due to doubts and self-perceptions of academic ability, antisocial behaviour, rejection from peers and/or a lack of educational preparation prior to entering the school in a refugee camp. School drop-outs may also be caused by unsafe school conditions, poverty, and so on.
- Social and individual rejection caused by hostile discrimination which in turn generates additional trauma when refugee children are treated cruelly by their peers.
- Identity confusion.
- Behavioural issues: caused by the adjustment issues and survival behaviours learned in refugee camps.

Conclusion

During her fieldwork in the Syrian refugee camps, the villages, the cities and Beirut in Lebanon, Nina experienced all of these variables associated with the provision of schooling – or lack of it – in the disrupted social and economic environments. It is a narrative of untold human sacrifice in the face of what are at times unimaginable odds. All Syrian families all Syrian parents and all Syrian children have their own stories.

The thought of being amongst refugees and sharing people lives and feelings with them instead of hearing about it via the media was overwhelming. Nina expressed mixed thoughts as the time for beginning her task approached. She did not know what to expect from her visits to certain areas, nor how people would react to yet another person asking more questions. She was uncertain about the stability of the whole political situation in Lebanon. These questions and others about the importance of speaking to refugees and locals and hearing the true stories of their survival and educational opportunities, were going through her mind.

References

American Near East Refugee Aid (ANERA). (2014). Stories: Lebanon. Retrieved 12 January 2015, from <http://www.anera.org/locations/lebanon/>.

Batha, E. (2013). Child marriage on rise among Syrian refugees-aid groups. *Thomson Reuters Foundation.* Retrieved 24 July 2014, from <http://www.trust.org/item/?map=child-marriage-on-rise-among-syrian-refugees-aid-groups/>.

Bridging Refugee Youth and Children's Services. (2006). *Educational handbook for refugee parents*. New York: International Rescue Committee.

Drumm, R. D., Pittman, S. W. & Perry, S. (2004). Social work interventions in refugee camps. *Journal of Social Service Research, 30*(2), 67–92. doi: 10.1300/J079v30n02_05.

Fazel, M. & Stein, A. (2002). The mental health of refugee children. *Archives of Diseases in Childhood, 87*(5), 366–370.

Gottfredson, D. C., Cook, P. J. & Na, C. (2011). School-based crime prevention. In B. C. Welsh & D. P. Farrington (Eds.), *The Oxford Handbook on Crime Prevention*. New York: Oxford University Press.

Lustig, S. L., Kia-Keating, M., Knight, W., Geltman, P., Ellis, H., Kinzie, J. D., Saxe, G. N. (2004). Review of child and adolescent refugee mental health. *Child and Adolescent Psychiatry, 43*(1), 24–36.

McCarthy, F. E. & Vickers, M. H. (2012). *Refugee and immigrant students: Achieving equity in education*. Charlotte, NC: Information Age Publishing.

Mulford, B., Kendall, D., Ewington, J., Edmunds, B., Kendall, L. & Silins, H. (2008.). Successful principalship of high-performance schools in high-poverty communities. *Journal of Educational Administration, 46*(4), 461–480.

Mwancha, D. (2014). Former Somali refugees raise funds in Canada to build pre-school in Dadaab. Retrieved 24 July 2014, from <http://www.unrefugees.org.au/news-and-media/news-headlines/kenya-former-somali-refugees-raise-funds-in-canada-to-build-pre-school-in-dadaab>.

Porter, M. & Haslam, N. (2005). Predisplacement and postdisplacement factors associated with mental health of refugees and internally displaced persons. *The Journal of the American Medical Association, 294*(5), 602–612.

Powell, A. (2014, 5 February). Perilous plight for Syrian refugees in Lebanon, child exploitation, illness among concerns cited by researchers. *Harvard Gazette.* Retrieved 16 December 2014, from <http://news.harvard.edu/gazette/story/2014/02/plight-of-syrian-refugees-in-lebanon-becoming-desperate/>.

Sidhu, R. & Taylor, S. (2012). Supporting refugee students in schools: what constitutes inclusive education? *International Journal of Inclusive Education, 16*(1), 39–56.

Simmons, A. (1985). *Immigration and Canada: Global and transnational perspectives*. Toronto, Ontario: Canadian Scholar's Press, Inc.

Thomas, C. M., Calvo, R. & Loughry, M. (2015). Refugee health and wellbeing: Differences between urban and camp-based environments in Sub-Saharan Africa. Retrieved from Journal of Refugee Studies website: <http://jrs.oxfordjournals.org/content/early/2015/04/15/jrs.fev003.short?rss=1 doi:10.1093/jrs/fev003>.

Taylor, J. (2004). Refugees and social exclusion: What the literature says. *Migration Action, 26*(2), 16–31.

United Nations High Commissioner for Refugees (UNHCR). (2009). UNHCR Policy on refugee protection and solution in urban areas. Retrieved 26 June 2015, from <http://www.unhcr.org/4ab356ab6.pdf>.

United Nations High Commissioner for Refugees (UNHCR). (2001). Learning for a future: Refugee education in developing countries. Retrieved 24 July 2014, from <http://www.unhcr.org/4a1d5ba36.html>.

Whyte, S. & Ting, I. (2014, 21 June). As world refugee numbers hit 50 million, Australia goes backwards. *Sydney Morning Herald.* Retrieved 24 July, 2014, from <http://www.smh.com.au/national/as-world-refugee-numbers-hit-50-million-australia-goes-backwards-20140620–3ajqj.html>.

Chapter Three
The Provision of Schooling and Challenges for Education for Refugees Inside and Outside Camps in Lebanon

Introduction

Syrian refugee children suffer from the lack of provision of schooling, as distinct from education. Families, peer groups, and various other informal networks provide some form of education to these children. This chapter draws a distinction between the meanings of the words "schooling" and "education", so as to highlight the suffering and negative influences for refugees in Lebanon, where large sections of the population are deprived of formal schooling. Schooling is culture-bound and not universally accepted. (On the other hand, all societies have developed systems of education, although the idea of the school came much later, and during the second part of the twentieth century it came under challenge).

This chapter also presents the Lebanese government's response plans in partnership with the UNHCR on schooling provisions and education schemes for refugee children.

Schooling and education

Schooling and education are not synonymous. Education happens even outside of schools. As in many developed countries, the notion of "schooling" is decidedly associated with paradigms of control and personality development within a formal setup. Schooling entails the implemention of a curricula that allows students to gain desired learning competencies that enable them to acquire a certificate at the culmination of schooling. It cannot be denied that sometimes, the most "schooled" happen to be the most "educated" as well, if not, the most successful in society. Likewise, there are those who are schooled, but come out uneducated. While education and success can happen even without schooling, the growing economic pressures of securing gainful employment amidst competition implies that schooling is important, relevant and inevitable in today's society.

There is increasing political interest in schooling outcomes and research is paying more attention to this topic. For example, one such research showed:

> Recent direct measures of the schooling-learning gap suggest that official literacy statistics significantly underestimate the scale of the problem. In several developing countries, many of the students who were enrolled in six full years of primary education were unable to answer questions about a simple paragraph or solve simple math problems. This suggests a dismal rate of return on years of school enrolment (Pritchett, Banerji & Kenny, 2013, p. 5).

While one can be educated without schooling, it must be realised that schooling provides other distinct advantages to individuals, much sought after by many refugee families seeking a better life. However, the delivery of a relevant and liberating schooling for refugee children remains a challenge.

Girls' schooling in developed and developing countries, even then, remains a challenge. Education through formal schooling is one of the most critical areas of empowerment, especially for women. It is also an area that offers some of the clearest examples of discrimination women suffer. Among children not attending school, there are twice as many girls as boys, and among illiterate adults, there are twice as many women as men.

Offering girls basic education through the formal process of schooling is one sure way of giving them much greater power – of enabling them to make genuine choices over the kinds of lives they wish to lead. Moreover, this is not a luxury. The Convention on the Rights of the Child and the Convention on the Elimination of All Forms of Discrimination against Women establish it as a basic human right.

According to a UNICEF (1996) report, women should have the opportunity to lead a healthier and happier life and this should be reason enough for promoting girls' education through formal schooling. However, there are also important benefits for the wider society as a whole. An educated woman has the skills, information and self-confidence she needs to be a better parent, worker and citizen. Moreover, an educated woman is likely to marry at a later age and have fewer children. Cross-country studies show that an extra year of schooling for girls reduces fertility rates by five per cent to ten per cent. Furthermore, the children of an educated mother are more likely to survive.

The seeds of segmented positive assimilation begin in refugee camps. According to Xie and Greenman (2011) "segmented assimilation refers to a variety of adaptive experiences immigrants may have as they become part of a host society" (p. 21). The authors show:

> The traditional model of assimilation involves four phases: contact, competition, accommodation, and then finally, assimilation. These phases were thought to be a common experience for all immigrants to a new host society. Segmented assimilation, however, includes many different ways that a new immigrant may adapt to a new society. They may follow the traditional model and assimilate into the white middle class. Alternatively, they might follow a less prosperous path and assimilate into the underclass. Finally, they might attain upward mobility in a tight-knit immigrant community (pp. 21–22).

Educational attainment through formal schooling vastly increases the opportunities for successful assimilation in another country. However, enabling the access to schooling, not to mention addressing socio-economic difficulties of refugees through employment and income support, will further allow successful assimilation.

Pedagogy of the displaced

Inspired by Paulo Freire's critical pedagogy (1970), this book attempts to present a concept of schooling refugee children. It is referred to as the "pedagogy of the displaced". This concept will be developed from the perspectives of refugee children, their parents, teachers, the community leaders of the displaced. While the host state and international agencies provide financial support, education and schooling for refugee children, it is expedient to understand and recognise the ability of the refugee community to advance the pedagogy of the displaced. The situations of the displaced are not predestined or permanent. It is socially constructed and can be addressed by the concerted efforts of not only the host and global communities, but also the displaced. It may be long-term but the struggle for liberation from economic helplessness and lack of social support has to happen. The dehumanising effect of war, conflict and dislocation on children has to be addressed. The authors have proposed that this pedagogy of the displaced is liberating, humanising, transforming and resilient. The refugee children face a reality that limits their potential every day and they risk becoming a lost generation. Education and schooling are achievable goals that can address this limitation both in the short-term and well into the future.

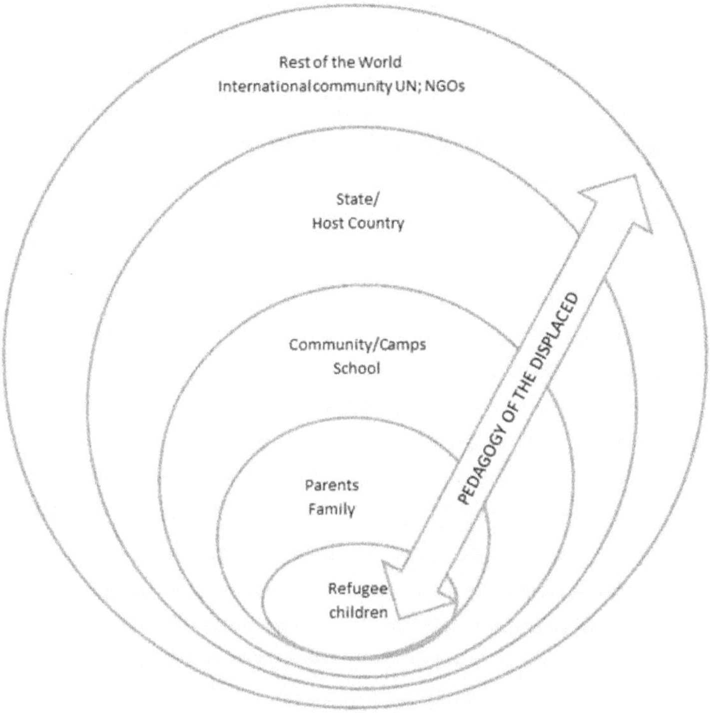

Figure 3: Dimensions informing the pedagogy of the displaced.

The research of Perumal (2013) on the pedadogy of refuge has particular relevance for this present book. In her research of displaced persons in South Africa, she emphasises the importance of postcolonial and deconstructionist conceptions of hospitality. As Nina travelled through Lebanon, she found much that would match with Perumal's (2013) research findings. Nina found the notion of hospitality, for students, teachers, principals and parents can be a two-edged sword – both liberating and constricting. Indeed, extrapolating from "postcolonial and deconstructionist sensibilities to explore how discourses on hospitality can provide a lens via which to engage education as an economy of hospitality", and also recruiting "insights offered by critical feminism as they relate to notions of communities of practice" as with Perumal (2013, p. 216) Nina found these liberating and restricting forces in the notion of the politics of hospitality.

Influenced by the research of Morrison and O'Gorman (2008, p. 216), Perumal (2013) found issues related to democracy, citizenship, social exclusion, xenophobia, and racism as revealing the "ethics and politics of hospitality and the status of the stranger, visitor, migrant, asylum seeker, and the refugee". (p. 677). Indeed, Perumal (2013) shows "deconstructionist theories, as popularised by Derrida (1998, 2000) conceive of hospitality as inviting and welcoming the "stranger"". We need to note "this invitation occurs on two levels: the personal level, where the "stranger" is welcomed into the home; and at the level of individual countries" (Perumal, 2013, p. 677). There is, however, an inherent tension in these notions of hospitality.

Following on from research by Derrida (2000), Perumal (2013) contends:

> the law of hospitality is a law of tension; a Janus-faced dialectic that contains two laws: conditional and unconditional. On the one hand, unconditional hospitality is a gracious act that is not performed out of duty. It expects nothing in return. It is a law without law, where the stranger turns into an awaited guest. This gesture of unconditional invitation is impossible without sovereignty of one-self over one's home. The stranger is welcomed as non-enemy. Ironically, one can become xenophobic in order to protect one's sovereignty, one's community of practice help define "who we are" both as a group and as individuals, but also "who we are," our particular identity, helps define the community of practice through the models of expertise, which develop … it is important to recognise the systematic and structural issues that mediate power relationships within communities of practice. This crucial issue has been mapped on the blind spot in the discourse on communities of practice (p. 678).

As Nina journeyed through Lebanon in her research quest, she encountered many instances substantiating these findings and as such, the pedagogy of the displaced has been developed.

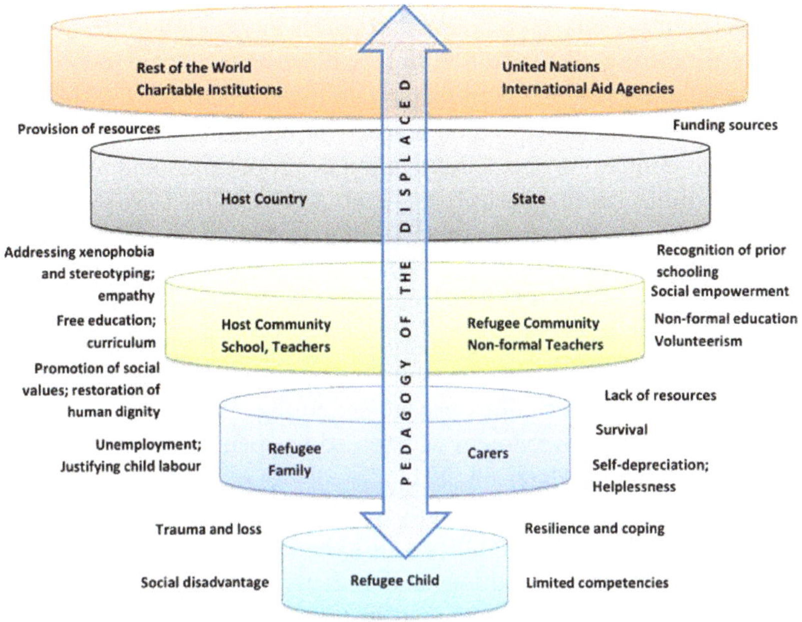

Figure 4: Conceptualising the pedagogy of the displaced.

Education in Lebanon

Lebanon enjoys one of the highest rates of literacy in the Arab world (97 per cent). It was estimated that in the late 1980's, the number of students in schools was over 80 per cent (UNHCR, 2013a). Regrettably, the civil war had a catastrophic effect on educational standards and the country's literacy rates. Amongst the issues contributing to the decline in academic standards, one of the most important was that while the Israeli raids destroyed over 150 schools, many families had to relocate to the remaining schools because their homes had been destroyed and they had nowhere else to go. The country also lost many teachers, professors and educators due to migration overseas. Furthermore, some schools were pressured by certain militias to enrol unqualified students. Along with this, many students lost their parents, their homes and access to schooling for a length of time, despite being allowed to return to achieve a designated level of education when much of the infrastructure had been destroyed. Finally, many schools were used as distribution centers for humanitarian aid (Mikdadi, 1983), or as centres for the dissemination of propaganda and recruitment of young soldiers to various militias (Brett & McCallin, 1996).

There are three systems of schooling in Lebanon: public schools, privately subsidized religiously affiliated schools and privately non-subsidized schools. Most Lebanese wish to enrol their children in private schools in the belief that they provide better education, discipline and etiquette. However, the poverty caused by the civil war ensured that many people could no longer afford private schooling. When the demand for education rose, the government was forced to open more public schools to meet this demand (Harrison, 2011).

Private schools depend heavily on numerous religious communities that have been long established in Lebanon and that have created a variety of educational institutions and systems. The diversity in religious schools varies from Western clerical institutions, to the Jesuits' schools that have existed in Lebanon since 1625, to the Presbyterian missionaries who started in 1866 and competed with the Catholics. Then there are the Makasids or Islamic schools, funded by the Gulf countries and Saudi Arabia. The Palestinians were not provided with public education in Lebanon until the United Nations Relief and Works Agency for Palestine Refugees in the Near East (UNRWA) was established and registered all Palestinian refugees in Lebanon, Syria, Jordan and Palestine (Ministry of Education and Higher Education, 2012). By 1975 the educational institutions in Lebanon were well entrenched. This situation contributed to the divisions and barriers that erupted into civil war.

Most parents stretch their budgets to the extreme to keep their children in private schools; a practice which is influenced by Lebanon's religious and internationalised culture, since most public schools are the object of criticism from Lebanese families. Yet, the education system in Lebanon is, to a reasonable extent, centralised and the same curriculum is taught in both private and public schools. Primary education is almost universal and covers Years 1–8, with an enrolment ratio of 95.4 per cent of the population. In secondary education the ratio reached 81.5 per cent in 2007 for Years 9–13 (UNESCO, 2008), while the adult literacy rate reached 88 per cent (UNICEF, 2004). Of the 112,111 students in schools in the country in 2009, 36,885 (30.29 per cent) were in public schools and the remaining number were in various levels of private schools.

The Lebanese Ministry of Education and Higher Education (MoEHE) has always controlled the education system through its licensing of private schools by enforcing requirements and regulations for graduates to comply with the Brevet Diploma (for graduating from middle school) and the Baccalaureate Diploma (for graduating after completing the final year of high school). An extra examination beyond the Baccalaureate, however, is required for entry to most of those institutions of higher education where the focus is on language competency, science and mathematics (Aljarida Alrasmiya, 1997).

In 1998 a reformed curriculum was launched with a focus on social, economic and national perspectives in which over 16,000 teachers were trained for public schools and 6,000 for private schools. The curriculum purported that twelve years were needed for schooling. It added one year to primary schooling, while removing one year from the middle years' cycle. History, geography, literature and civics are still being taught in Arabic, while all other subjects are taught in either English or French, depending on the school's educational and religious background.

Post-civil war developments

Notwithstanding the reform of the curriculum, improvements in teacher preparation, and development in most areas of education, many aspects of Lebanon's education system remain problematic and continue to compromise students' results and their future success. UNICEF (2004) documented that at least fifteen per cent of students in Lebanese schools had dropped out and another eleven per cent had to repeat their year level. Research shows that the war left public schools with inadequate equipment and facilities to support students, while private schoolss fees went up to re-build and re-stock. This left many parents financially struggling and resulted in many students having to drop out. These results were confirmed by the United Nations Human Rights Council (2006), which stated that as a consequence of the loss of over 180 school buildings in southern

Lebanon and southern suburbs of Beirut due to Israeli air strikes, more than 300 schools needed major repairs. It was also emphasized that teachers needed to take account of the psychological effects of the war on children and their parents (UNICEF, 2007).

The Lebanese people are also segregated by the education system itself (Hajjar, 2002). According to Hajjar (2002), the three different sectors of schooling – French, British and American – have led to community division where they should have been unity at a time when their relationships with each other and the communities have been deeply scarred by the civil war. History, with its variegated interpretations, is still taught in different versions within different school sectors, indicating that the civil war is being interpreted along sectarian lines (Euro News, 2011in Maadad, 2013), even though the Ministry of Education formulated an agreement whereby all school sectors use a common history book. Unfortunately, and to the detriment of children who study the subject, Lebanese politicians and community leaders continue to disagree and refuse to compromise (European Neighbourhood and Partnership Instrument, 2007). The latest attempt at reconciliation was a meeting to release a new book titled *Learning and Teaching History: Lessons from and for Lebanon* (Ghusayni *et al.*, 2012) at the Ministry of Education and Higher Education, where most school sector leaders and university history advisors as well as representatives from the UNESCO met to discuss the possibilities of writing a new common school history book (Ministry of Education and Higher Education, 2012).

Most schools have their own "hidden curriculum" (Toronto & Eissa, 2007, p. 28), which is reflected in their ethos, teachers, community services and religious activities. A study undertaken by Abouchedid *et al.* (2002) contended that prototypes of political socialisation strongly influence the religious agenda in Lebanon, including in schools. Their study focused on the teaching of history in the different school sectors and reported that seven different history textbooks were used. Each presented elements of the country's history which interpreted past events in terms politically acceptable to one section of the community. Also, political propaganda is often prevalent in private, subsidised private and public schools, being related to the ideas of the particular party, or militia, that provides them with support, protection and finance (Cervan, 2011). The only schools in which political topics cannot be discussed are the Hariri schools.

Syrian and Syrian Palestinian education in Lebanon

Prior to the outbreak of the 2011 political crisis and armed conflict in Syria, children enjoyed an almost universal education in that country, in which literacy rate for Syrian youths aged 15–24 was more than 90% (Save the Children, 2015). With the enactment of Syria's Compulsory Education Law No. 35 of 1981, which made education compulsory for all Syrian children and their peers (e.g., Palestinians living in Syria) from Years 1–6, and the 2002 Basic Education Law No. 32, which streamlined the elementary and primary education into one basic stage of education starting from Year 1 till Year 9, the Ministry of Education had centralised Syria's educational system under its supervision, providing educational services to fourteen directorates and provinces. The Ministry of Education had set the curriculum, the goals of teaching and the approach to the interaction of teaching, learning and the curricula, as well as the production of curricular support materials that provided information about various teaching methods (Abouawn, 2012). The medium of instruction is exclusively in Arabic.

A three year pre-primary schooling was offered to children aged three to five but was not compulsory nor free. Schooling was compulsory and free for all children from the age of six until twelve, and all schoolbooks were free. Most primary schools (98%) were run by the government and less than two per cent were private schools while less than half per cent were run by UNRWA. All schools followed the curriculum provided by the Ministry of Education (Abouawn, 2012). The curriculum covered Arabic, mathematics, religious instruction, elements of science and health education, social and national education, art, music and physical education. Schooling for children included six years of compulsory primary (Years 1 to 6), which lasted for five hours per day (four hours in some rural areas) for 200 days in a given school year.

Three years of compulsory lower secondary schooling is being provided at no cost, to children aged 12 to 14. This preparatory or intermediate schooling had a curriculum consisting of all the subjects taught at primary level with the addition of languages (English and French) and "female education". A qualifying examination for the Intermediate Level Diploma was given at the end of Year 9. From aged 14 to 18, students could undergo another three years of upper secondary education (Years 10 to 12), if their results in the competitive entry examination for a diploma were high enough. Secondary schools for the upper levels provided either general or vocational curricula. The general curriculum prepared the students for university entrance, while the vocational curriculum allowed them for entry into viable trades and work. Within this structure, increased attention to technical education was met. Students received a Technical Baccalaureate upon completion. Secondary schools are open to all primary school students wishing to continue their education. Upon completion of upper secondary school under a general curriculum, the students sit for the Secondary Diploma (Baccalaureate), which is the sole qualification to grant automatic entrance to universities and other institutions of higher education. Higher education students attended the universities at Damascus, Aleppo, Latakia, and Homs.

At the time of the writing of this book, war had decimated Syria's educational institutions, displacing more than two million children (Craissati, 2015; UNICEF, 2015; UNHCR, 2014b; UNESCO, 2013; Abouawn, 2012) who have found refuge in countries such as Lebanon, Jordan, Iran, Egypt and Turkey.

Politics of education for the Syrian refugees in Lebanon

Lebanon now hosts more than 1.5 million refugees from Syria, and of this figure, fifty-three per cent are children under the age of 18 (UNHCR, 2014c). Close to 800,000 school-age children are in need of education assistance in Lebanon. At the time of the writing of this book, less than fifteen per cent are enrolled in formal basic education (UNICEF, 2015). The Lebanese Ministry of Education and Higher Education (MoEHE) had earlier expressed that with its current state, it can only accommodate 90,000 children in its public school system, but not without capacity support from the international community (UNHCR, 2014c). In this current situation, a great number of Syrian children face limited opportunities for the future and risk higher exposure to economic and social disadvantages.

Thirty per cent of Lebanese school-age children are in the public schools while seventy percent go to private schools. Lebanon hosts more school-age refugees than the entire intake of the country's public school

(Craissati, 2015). This has strained Lebanon's already ailing public school system that faces numerous problems such as insufficient funding, lack of sanitation facilities and limited library books and science laboratory facilities (Cochran, 2014).

The curriculum has been a political issue ever since the Lebanese school system has taken in children refugees from Syria. Nirrengarten, the education officer with UNHCR in Lebanon explained in an interview in the *Al-Monitor* that the MoEHE "did not want to get involved in the politics of the Syrian curriculum or create a new version exclusively for them" (Kangarlou, 2015, p. 2). One area of contention is the legitimacy of the Syrian government providing the Syrian curriculum. In Turkey, the Syrian National Coalition (SNC), government-in-exile, has been recognised in 2013, and there, the curriculum developed by the SNC Government is being used for the children who have fled Syria into Turkey. Lebanese authorities have been very cautious of implementing anything similar as they do not wish to be involved in Syrian politics nor school curriculum.

Moreover, there are other issues that face school-age children refugees from Syria. Kangarlou (2015, p. 1) reported:

> Curriculum complexities, language barriers, cultural divides, financial difficulties, bullying, exclusion of those with physical and mental disabilities and distance to schools are some of the factors preventing Syrian and Lebanese children alike from accessing education.
>
> In Syria, teaching is exclusively in Arabic, while in Lebanon – depending on the school – some courses are taught in English or French. This is a particular problem for older children and those who have missed a few years of school due to displacement.

Given the difficulties faced by the Lebanese public school system, the MoEHE has launched a three-year programme to address such difficulties impinging on not only the Lebanese school-age children but also the children refugees from Syria. Dubbed as "Reaching All Children with Education", the programme aimed to enrol more than 400,000 children by 2016. This programme provided for a second shift for schooling in public schools for Syrian children. The "Accelerated Learning Programme" is another strategy that the MoEHE developed to address the learning needs of Syrian children, who have missed more than one year of schooling, with the aim of intensively catching up on coursework (Kangarlou, 2015;

UNICEF, 2015). The MoEHE will manage these programmes' funds, which will be provided by UN agencies and other donors.

The UNHCR responds to the unfolding crisis

Maria Calivis (in Craissati, 2014), UNICEF's regional director for the Middle East and Africa, reported early in the year that UNICEF is providing psychological and educational support for most refugees but more resources would be needed to cover the large number of people. She mentioned in her statement that only twenty-five per cent of children were enrolled in schools. Syrian refugee children according to UNHCR were not responding in a positive way to kindergarten, and in terms of primary education level, they comprised almost half of the total number of school-age children, a total of 275,850 (UNESCO, 2013a).

Calivis proposed reasons such as; students' inability to integrate back into school after a long break; safety; and parents' inability to afford the cost of schooling and lack of transport. The biggest challenge, she explained, was the fact that schools are full and teachers are under pressure. (Calivis in Craissati, 2014).

According to UNHCR (2014a), legal regulations in Lebanon as they apply to education, mandate the responsibility of providing a safe environment for all children. However, regardless of such regulations, there have been many complaints about teachers and principals mistreating Syrian children enrolled in public schools. During Nina's visits to schools and while talking to students and parents, she was informed that some children experience physical and verbal abuse from their teachers, and many reported that their peers also bullied them in and out of schools. However, she was also informed the children and their parents would never complain publicly or report these incidents to authorities because they feared losing their places in schools.

Nina's visits covered schools in many regions of Lebanon including the north, Bekaa Valley and Zahle, the middle (Matn area), the centre of the capital city Beirut as well as areas in the south-west. Some of these schools were located inside refugee camps, while many others were not.

Figure 5: The Political Map of Lebanon helps the user in getting a clear idea about the various parts of Lebanon. This map shows international boundary, the state boundaries with their capitals, national capital and other important cities.

Conclusion

For decades now, international media has been reporting the tragedy of the world's refugees. No country remains unaffected. As with the now well-known butterfly effect, a butterfly flutters its wings in Syria or Lebanon, and it is felt in far-off countries such as Australia, in some way or another. A family shivers with trauma in the Bekaa Valley and Zahle, children are forced to go without formal education in one of the many refugee camps in this area, and there is some kind of repercussion in some other part of the world.

Schooling and education generally is important for the refugee children, but even more important is certified achievement in formal school education. Schools and qualified school teachers, who implement a recognised curriculum, constitute the valued conduit for a better life. These were some of the concerns harboured by Nina when she set off for her home country to talk with various people and groups concerned with schooling for the refugee children and young adults.

Syrian refugee children are like all other children worldwide; to list few things only – the children need families, friends, homes, schools, playgrounds, toys, books, food, dreams, freedom, happiness, love, stability, good health facilities, good nutrition and safety. They need to live their childhood and they have the right to embrace all the things in the list above. Most of the children, who Nina met have very few of the things on the list and some have hardly any thing.

References

Abouchedid, K., Nasser, R. & Blommestein, J. (2002). The limitations of inter-group learning in confessional school systems: the case of Lebanon. *Arab Studies Quarterly*, Vol.24, no.4, pp.61–74.

Aljarida Alrasmiya of the Republic of Lebanon. (1977). *Laws and decrees concerningt he pre-university educational system*. Beirut: Sader Publications.

Brett, R. & McCallin, M. (1996). *Children: The invisible soldiers*. Stockholm: Sewdish Save the Children.

Cervan, D. (2011). Religion in education and conflict: Lebanon and Northern Ireland compared. Retrieved 21 January 2014, from <https://www.ruor.uottawa.ca/bitstream/10393/20006/1/Cervan_Daniel_2011_thesis.pdf>.

Derrida, J. (2000) "Hospitality", *Angelaki: Journal of the Theoretical Humanities*, Vol. 5, no. 3, pp. 3–18.

European Neighbourhood and Partnership instrument. (2007). *Lebanese Republic: Country Strategy and National Indicative Program*. Belguim: European External Action Service.

Ghusayni, R., Akkary, R.K. & Akar, B. (2012). *Learning and teaching history: Lessons from and for Lebanon*. Beirut: Lebanese Association for Educational Studies.

Hajjar, G. (2002). *Aspects of Christian -Muslim relations in contemporary Lebanon*. Lebanon: Notre Dame University.

Harrison, K. (2011). Between politics and identity: The history and future of education in Lebanon. Retrieved 12 January 2015, from <www.tuftsgloballeadership.or/files/between_politics_identity.pdf>.

Maadad, N. (2013). Lebanon: Post civil war implications for schools. In S. R. P. Clarke & T. A. O'Donoghue (Eds.), *School-level leadership in post- conflict societies* (pp. 127–144). Oxon; New York: Taylor & Francis.

Mikdadi, L. (1983). *Surviving the siege of Beirut: A personal account*. London: Onyx Press.

Ministry of Education and Higher Education of Lebanon. (2005). Retrieved 12 January 2015, from <http://www.crdp.rof/CRDP/Arabic/ar-statistics/STAT>.

Ministry of Education and Higher Education of Lebanon. (2012). Retrieved 12 January 2015, from <http://www.crdp.rof/CRDP/Arabic/ar-statistics/STAT>.

Morrison, A., and K. O'Gorman (2008) "Hospitality Studies and Hospitality Management: A Symbiotic Relationship", *International Journal of Hospitality Management*, Vol. 27, pp. 214–221.

Perumal, J. C. (2013). Pedagogy of refuge: education in a time of dispossession. *Race Ethnicity and Education, 16*(5), 673–695.

Save the Children. (2015). *Small hands, heavy burden: How the Syria conflict is driving more children into the workforce*. London: Save the Children; UNICEF.

Toronto, J. & Eissa, M. (2007). Egypt: Promoting tolerance, defending against Islamism. In E. Abdellah & G. Starrett (Eds.), *Teaching Islam* (pp. 27–51). London: Lynne Reinner Publishers.

United Nations Educational, Scientific & Cultural Organization (UNESCO). (2013). Syrian refugees education: Country profile. Retrieved 7 July 2015, from <http://www.unesco.org/new/fileadmin/MULTIMEDIA/FIELD/Beirut/images/Lebanon_Country_Profile.pdf>.

United Nations Educational, Scientific & Cultural Organization (UNESCO). (2008). Institute for statistics database. Retrieved 12 January 2015, from <www.uis.unesco.org>.

United Nations High Commissioner for Refugees (UNHCR). (2014c). Barriers to education for Syrian refugee children in Lebanon. Retrieved 10 April 2015, from <http://www.proasyl.de/fileadmin/proasyl/fm_redakteure/Newsletter _Anhaenge/207/reach_lbn_report_syriacrisis_outofschoolchildrenprofiling_nov2014.pdf>.

United Nations High Commissioner for Refugees (UNHCR). (2014a). 2014 Syria regional resopnse plan: Education. *Vulnerability Assessment for Syrian Refugees (VASyR), WFP, UNHCR, UNICEF.* Retrieved 14 July 2015, from <http://www.unhcr.org/syriarrp6/midyear/index.html>.

United Nations High Commissioner for Refugees (UNHCR). (2014b). Syrian refugee crisis- inter-agency regional update. Retrieved 24 January 2015, from <www.data.unhcr.org/syrianrefugees/regional.php>.

United Nations High Commissioner for Refugees (UNHCR). (2013a). The challenge of education: The future of Syria refugee children in crisis. Retrieved 20 September 2014, from <http://www.unhcr.org/syria/the-challenge-of-education>.

United Nations Human Rights Council. (2006). Resolution adopted by the General Assembly on 15 March 2006. Retrieved 12 January 2015, from <http://www.daccess-dds-ny.un.org>.

United Nations International Children's Emergency Fund (UNICEF). (2015). Syria crisis monthly humanitarian highlights & results. *#Children of Syria*. Retrieved 22 August 2015, from <http://childrenofsyria.

info/2015/06/30/syria-crisis-monthly-humanitarian-highlights-results-may-2015-syria-jordan-lebanon-iraq-turkey-and-egypt/>.

United Nations International Children's Emergency Fund (UNICEF). (2007). The humanitarian action report. Retrieved 12 January 2015, from <www.unicef.org/har07/index.html>.

United Nations International Children's Emergency Fund (UNICEF). (2004). The state of the world's children. Retrieved 12 January 2015, from <www.unicef.org/sowc04>.

United Nations International Children's Emergency Fund (UNICEF). (1996). Girls' education: A lifeline to development. *The State of the World's Children.* Retrieved 12 March 2015, from <http://www.unicef.org/sowc96/ngirls.htm>.

Xie, Y. & Greenman, E. (2011). The social context of assimilation: testing implications of segmented assimilation theory. *Social Science Research, 40*(3), 965–984.

Chapter Four
Children's Experiences

Nina visited schools in villages, in camps; she visited formal public schools and non-formal school, and two private schools, where she managed to obtain responses to questions about schooling experiences. She started her visits in the north, specifically the Bekaa Valley and travelled through the middle of the country towards Beirut initially, and then to the south-west. The availability of education to children varies largely from one area to another and from one school to the next.

Child brides: "one less mouth to feed"

Emma Batha (2013) from Reuters reported a horrific outcome of this unfolding tragedy: "the desperate plight of refugees fleeing Syria's civil war is forcing some parents to marry off their daughters as child brides, aid workers warn" (Batha, 2013, n.p.). Bath went on to report that according to Refugees International, "in some cases, landlords in Jordan were exploiting the situation by offering to waive a family's rent in exchange for marrying their daughter" (Batha, 2013, n.p.). According to Batha (2013) the young girls and their families were being exploited. She further pointed out:

> There are also reports of men from Saudi Arabia and other Middle Eastern countries looking for young Syrian brides among refugee communities. Aid workers believe some of the marriages are temporary, so-called pleasure marriages – short-term arrangements for money (Batha, 2013, n.p.).

Batha (2013, n.p.) also noted "a report by aid agency MercyCorps on refugees in Jordan said U.N. and Jordanian relief agencies estimated some 500 underage Syrians were wed last year [2012]." Batha (2013) reported that according to MercyCorps early marriages of girls cause serious health and wellbeing issues. Girls who marry young have their education cut short and are more likely to suffer domestic violence. Indeed, for MercyCorps, according to Batha (2013, n.p.) "refugees marrying off underage daughters were not bad parents, but that they simply felt there was no alternative."

When Sarah Dingle (2014) interviewed Paul Ronalds, Chief Executive of Save the Children, for the Australian Broadcasting Commission's *The World Today* program on 17 July 2014, many Australians were horrified to learn this catastrophe had grown. According to Ronalds:

> Previously in 2011, when the humanitarian crisis in Syria was just beginning, it was around 12 per cent. That went up to about eighteen per cent in 2012 and now is around 25 per cent of all girl children under 18 (in Dingle, 2014, n.p.).

Approximately one quarter of all Syrian child refugees in Jordan, girl children, were being married before the age of 18 (Dingle, 2014, n.p.). Ronalds added:

> Just the sheer scale of the humanitarian crisis in Syria, and now in neighbouring Iraq and its impacting obviously on Lebanon and Jordan itself, creates the environment where families are struggling to cope and respond … The maths are not hard to do. We're seeing an absolute epidemic of child marriage in that environment (in Dingle, 2014, n.p.).

The UNHCR had well-researched evidence concerning the calamitous ramifications such events had for young adolescent girls in refugee camps. For example, in a 2001 report the UNHCR reported:

> Displaced communities are normally anxious to reintroduce schooling quickly, as soon as food and shelter are provided. They ask their educated members to start classes for the younger children on a voluntary basis. In many cases people fled without their belongings, so that it is difficult for classes to begin without external assistance. A flexible approach is needed so that students who were in upper primary and secondary school or higher education can also maintain and develop their study skills. There are various ways of doing this, such as involving youth in helping with younger children for part of the time and providing interim courses in languages or other subjects to maintain their study skills until they can resume their courses of study (p. 20).

Moreover, the 2001 UNHCR report emphasised "Rapid intervention of this kind is important, so that the benefit of past schooling is not lost and time is not wasted" (p. 20). Time is short for many of these children, especially girls, who as we have shown above, often have to leave school at puberty or early marriage, and boys from poor families, who have to work full-time as soon as they are old enough to do so. "Trauma can have a negative impact on study skills, as can a long gap in studies. Hence, the restoration of some kind of studies is urgent" (UNHCR, 2001, p. 20).

The 2001 UNHCR report went on to argue:

> Restoration of schooling brings the widely recognized benefits of schooling as such, including its contribution to productivity and economic development. It can contribute to social stability through engaging young people in sustained constructive activity. There are also long-term implications for social cohesion: it is undesirable for one group of the population to be severely under-educated relative to other groups, especially when there is an ethnic dimension. Schooling for girls leads to lower child and maternal mortality rates and increased female participation in economic and political decision-making (p. 20).

Clearly, schooling serves many purposes other than individual education. Refugees' fears and aspirations come to the surface as they recognise schooling can open the door to get out from the camp. That particular certificate, diploma or degree at the end of one's schooling for many individuals is a life-changing event, as the UNHCR (2001) report recognised:

> When refugees have been in exile for many years and a system of primary and secondary education has been established, then the situation is different. In this case, careful planning is needed to ensure that education is quickly developed in returnee areas, or to allow older students to complete their courses before repatriating, so that students are not cut off in the middle of a course of studies (UNHCR, 2001, p. 24).

Living conditions in the camps

Emphasising the point raised in the UNHCR (2001) report is a report to the *Harvard Gazette,* where Powell (2014) mentioned the living conditions vary widely from one area to another for Syrian refugees in Lebanon. Many refugees are not registered, and this does not help their situation in receiving support and assistance from aid agencies. The report also sparked a concern in relation to children under the age of eighteen, and the risk of working conditions that they get involved into, such as slave labour, sex trafficking, marriage for convenience and survival sex (Powell, 2014). Ronald Schilling (cited in Lynch & Faek, 2014, n.p.) a representative of the UNHCR to the United Kingdom, said in a statement reported in Al-Fanar media: "Ensuring that these young people have access to quality education while they are refugees is essential in addressing this urgent challenge".

A large number of Syrian children are already traumatised having to live in a war zone and witnessing violence, blood and death prior to their escape to neighbouring countries. Now these children have to miss out on a normal childhood filled with freedom and joy, and instead are forced to become the family's breadwinner and immerse themselves in life's catastrophic cruelty and depression (Grant & Harper, 2013, p. 6).

At every turn in the camps, there are the foul fruits of traumatised children. For example, Richard Spencer (2015) from the (London) *Telegraph* reported:

> A photographer working in a refugee camp in Syria unexpectedly found a little girl surrendering to him after he pointed his lens at her.
>
> The little girl, whose father had been killed in the conflict, raised her arms in fear when she saw the journalist, Osman Sağırlı.
>
> The picture of the little girl was published in Mr Sağırlı's Turkiye newspaper in January, but was tweeted by another journalist based in Gaza this week.
>
> Since then it has been retweeted tens of thousands of times.

One can only imagine the horror existing in the poor child's mind. Of course, one may suppose that is the case for refugees being repatriated from the camps. This applies as well to primary and secondary education, and not only tertiary education.

Despite refugee students valuing schooling and education as an agent for change, they may find that success in school will elude them. In fact they may encounter other obstacles, and these are as follows. First, there is the issue of disrupted schooling. Refugee children may experience disruptive schooling in their country of origin or an absence of schooling altogether. Teachers will agree that it is extremely difficult for students with no previous education to go into a classroom with educated children. Secondly, school dropouts emerge as a problem. It arises due to doubts and self-perceptions about academic ability, antisocial behaviour, rejection from peers and/or a lack of educational preparation prior to entering the school in a refugee camp. Unsafe school conditions, poverty, and so on, may cause school dropouts. Thirdly, social and individual rejection is caused by hostile discrimination, which in turn creates additional trauma when refugee children are treated cruelly by their peers. This can have implications for identity confusion. Fourthly, behavioural issues become a major concern, and they are caused by adjustment issues and survival behaviours learned in refugee camps.

The following questions focus on Syrian refugee children's responses to education and schooling in the regions we visited. They include villages, camps, four formal public schools outside the camps, two formal public schools inside the camps, two private schools and two non-formal schools. Nina started her visits in the north, specifically the Bekaa Valley and travelled through the middle of the country towards Beirut initially and then to the country's south-west. Children's access to education or its availability to them varies largely from one area to another and from one school to another.

Winter in the camps

Many Australians were as shocked, as we were, on viewing reports of sub-zero winter conditions in the Syrian refugee camps in Lebanon's Bekaa Valley in the early weeks of January 2015. This was our response to the story filed by the BBC's Paul Wood when he visited one makeshift camp. Many of the refugees lacked adequate clothing for the freezing weather, as Paul Wood (2015) reports:

> A snow storm in the Middle East is adding to the misery of the three million refugees who have fled the conflict Syria.
>
> The snow was falling thick and fast. The mountains on the border with Syria were wreathed in freezing mist and barely visible.
>
> Refugees were desperately sweeping snow off their tent roofs to stop them from collapsing.
>
> "There is no wood, no bread: it's hopeless," said Omar al-Mohammed.
>
> He complained bitterly that the refugees had seen their food rations cut - but the UN is desperately overstretched.
>
> "The children are hungry," he added. "We call upon the outside world to help us." …
>
> The camp's "main street" was a lake of slush and icy water. A little girl who looked about 10 years old was frantically trying to sweep the water away from the entrance to her tent.
>
> Some children were able to enjoy the snow despite not having suitable clothing and footwear
>
> She had only open sandals on her bare feet. Other children ran around, more dressed for summer than winter (n.p.).

Nina's visit to the Bekka Valley began with a serendipitous moment. This started in an encounter with Joumana.

Joumana from the Bekaa Valley

Only a few months earlier, during a warmer season, Nina visited a camp in the Bekaa Valley and spoke with Joumana, a beautiful nine-year old, about her classroom conditions. She goes to a non-formal school in the camp. As with many nine-year olds around the world, she was excited and swelled with self-importance to think that an important Australian university lecturer would be taking an interest in her school.

"How do you find your classroom?" Nina asked. Joumana became thoughtful, responding:

> The learning area that we sit in is beautiful in the summer and we can spread out and write comfortably. Sometimes we even do stretching exercises and we can also sleep on the mats on the floor after lunch but the room that we use in winter is very cold most of the time, so, we sit together to cuddle up until the teacher tells us off.

Months later, when reflecting on Paul Wood's (2015) BBC report, we had a vivid impression of what Joumana and her classmates had to contend with in winter. In the report Omar al-Mohammed spoke out against the cuts in food rations, and how the UNHCR was outstretched in its provisions for people in the camps. We need to remember, also, however, that these school provisions were as sparse as the flimsy tents Paul Woods' (2015) BBC report portrayed, of desperate people scraping away thirty or more centimeters of snow from their tents.

The human spirit, schooling and its physical provisions

As stated earlier, schools are not synonymous with physical school buildings. As the UNHCR (2001) puts it:

> Some people imagine that rapid education response means "building schools", but emergency education [schooling] frequently takes place under trees or plastic sheeting. School construction may happen later, in months or years (and by then, formal education would have started anyway). The argument that emergency education means "building schools" and will give a "feeling of permanence", is thus unrealistic (p. 24).

Rita Daou (2014) for *Yahoo News* reported on the physical provisions of the Lebanese Syrian refugee camps:

> Qaraun (Lebanon) (AFP) – In a squalid camp in eastern Lebanon, a school in a tent with a chalkboard and brightly coloured desks offers children who fled Syria's war a chance of an education.
>
> Thousands of child refugees are studying at dozens of makeshift schools across Lebanon, including 11-year old Faruq Salkhadi, who dreams of becoming a doctor.
>
> "It had been a year since I was last in school. My parents didn't have the money to pay school fees here in Lebanon for my three sisters and me," said Faruq, who is learning English, maths and Arabic.
>
> His tent school in the Qaraun area of the eastern Bekaa valley is one of 47 learning centres supervised by the International Rescue Committee (IRC) in the north and east of Lebanon.
>
> Faruq's family fled their hometown of Jassem, in the southern Syrian province of Daraa, after their two-storey house was bombed.
>
> They are now among more than 1.1 million Syrian refugees living in neighbouring Lebanon.

Again, more positively, and reflecting on Joumana's enthusiastic responses to Nina's questions about the schooling she received under harsh conditions, the strength of the human spirit prevailed. Clearly, here in the camps, it is the process of having students working with a teacher in a relatively planned and structured manner, complying with acceptable standards. This is schooling, taking its first tentative steps towards individual growth and community building.

Salem and Mohsin

Yet, as is the case in classrooms around the world, individuals will respond differently. Nina spoke with Salem, a young boy aged seven, with a a different outlook on schooling, who responded:

> We are so lucky to have a classroom; my mum says because the area that my cousins are living in is very bad and they don't have schools. I think that they are lucky because they don't have to go to school from a young age.

Then, for Nina, there was Mohsin, an eleven-year old happy enough to be able to attend school after missing out on two years of education. He thought that the classroom was very basic but provided them with enough space to generate education. One child aged thirteen who was attending a public school in the Bekaa Valley commented on this situation by saying that the classroom is nice but they are not allowed to use the same facilities that local children do, because the government cannot provide books and computers to all. The Lebanese children have priority. In her interviews with students, Nina notes few students who are living in the Bekaa Valley camps and attending schools in the camps talk about their dreams of having bigger rooms with lights and heating. Yet, some do confess to dreaming and talking about the ideal school that they hope they could one day attend. They say they would like to see a small playground outside their classroom, and to be able to play like they used to in their old schools back home in Syria.

Alia from Matn; Jamila from the Zahle area; and Abdou and Sanaa

The human spirit is strong, resurgent and responding to people's desire to improve their own learning environment. For Nina, Alia who attends a public school in the Matn area is the most vibrant and smallest eight-year old she had ever seen. Alia had such large and widely open bright hazel eyes, which surely would not have time to twitch, so they did not miss out on anything. Alia confessed she likes to decorate her classroom walls with her drawings to hide the holes and bricks which makes everyone happier. Similarly, Jamila is a little girl who goes to school in the Zahle area with her three siblings; they are all between seven and twelve years of age. She enjoyed telling Nina her classroom is so colourful and beautiful and that the classrooms of her sister and two brothers are also very bright, stimulating and comforting.

Nina reported the Salameh kids who attended the same school as Jamila also gave a brief and positive feedback about their views of their classrooms and were so excited to be able to attend the school because in the previous year there was not enough room to accommodate all Syrian refugees in the district. Similar to the Zahle children in the three schools Nina visited in the Matn area, located in the centre of Lebanon, the students were very content with the physical provisions of their respective schools, describing their classrooms with a positive outlook saying that they were modern and large. One child aged thirteen years who asked to remain anonymous – Nina gave him the name Abdou – is currently attending a private religious school.

Abdou explained their classroom is far better than his neighbour's who goes to a public school. Here in Abdou's school they have so many gadgets to use in the classroom. Children bring their own ipads or laptops if they want to use them in class. Another child named Sanaa, eleven years of age and attending the same private school, explained that their classroom is very comfortable. Nina, however, was aware of the fees her parents had to pay, and expected the room to be comfortable and accommodating.

Matn children excited about their classrooms

When Nina asked students who attend public schools in the north what they thought about their classroom, responses were also similar to those Nina received in the Matn area. The children are mostly excited and appreciative of having schools to attend. Soummaya who is a fifteen-year old and a refugee girl from a small village in Syria, explained the room is enough to allow her to provide some help and assistance to the primary school teacher with the extra refugee children in class. Soummaya did not attend school because there is none available in her area; even if they did have room for her, she would not be able to pay the fees. Soummaya, therefore, seems happy enough volunteering at the school to keep her mind active.

When Nina asked children attending the schools in the Zahle area about their respective institution's physical facilities, their responses were totally different. These children were attending public schools with Lebanese local students. When Nina spoke to the children about their needs and what they would like to have if they were given the opportunity, most of them wanted to be able to go back to their homes in Syria. Mona told Nina that she misses the garden and the roses that her mum used to take care of while she sat on the swing and sang songs for her mother. Mona was saddened by having lost her own room and now having to share a room not just with her siblings but also with her three cousins. "They all sleep on mattresses on the floor and it can be suffocating at times especially the many feet smell after a long day or after a warm lentil soup dinner" (Mona said while giggling). She explained that being in this situation made her appreciate what she once had back home in Syria; now that she shares a mattress, shares clothes, shares shoes and sometimes even has to sacrifice food to allow others in her family have something to eat.

Rida and Houda (Magida's children) took their time reflecting before answering Nina's question about their needs. Being older and wiser at the age of eleven, Houda said with a few tears in her eyes that her wish list would be so long at the moment if she were offered that option. Her wish list, she added, would consist of loads of happiness for her parents, who have been so depressed and unhappy in the last few years. She would want her aunt and uncle to be alive again and her parents to be surrounded with family and loved ones. Houda mentioned her dreams were shattered the day she watched her parents weep as they were leaving their hometown. She said one day she would write a story about her parents' life and the miseries that the civil war caused them and many like them. Rida, her younger nine-year old brother focused on materialistic needs that their family could do with; he said that his wish is for his father and mother to get some financial help so they do not need to work so hard. Rida showed Nina his sandals that he wears to school and shares with his younger brother when he is at home. He mentioned that his feet freeze in them in winter especially on the snow and asked Nina if she can imagine how cold his feet would be without them. Rida smiled and said that he wishes one day he does not have to share everything with everyone around him.

Children reflected with sadness on their needs and wishes for things they dream of having. Even though there were similarities in the answers given, there were few that were emotionally targeted; they were based on feelings and losses. Like Mayssoun the twelve-year old who wanted the friends she had while living in Syria. She narrated to Nina a story based on the lack of having someone she trusted to talk to, without having to add more troubles to the daily unhappiness for her parents. She wanted to share her thoughts with her friends about her worries and fears concerning her parents, who she often caught crying since their arrival to Lebanon. Zeina who will turn thirteen in a few months' time wished for peace in Syria so they can leave the Bekaa Valley and return home. She wanted to go back to her big family house and live next door to her grandparents and uncles and be spoiled and loved endlessly like she once did. Zeina admitted she gets envious watching the Lebanese girls from next door run and scream with excitement when they see their relatives pull into the drive way; she wishes she could see her extended family from Syria and spend time with them. She said that she is that desperate that she would not mind sharing the relatives like she shares books and clothes with her sisters.

"Our camp is like a sardine can"

Sociologists and town planners have long understood the debilitating effect of the physical environment on the human psyche. Despite the brave optimism revealed in the above student interviews, we need to recognise the problems caused by crowded environments in the refugee camps. The world's media has reported many times about the crowded life in Lebanon's refugee camps for displaced Syrians. Health care was critical. For example, James Meikle (2013) wrote in *The Guardian* on the "crowded, insanitary conditions and broken health system [were] expected to cause hepatitis, typhoid, cholera or dysentery" (n.p.) in the camps:

With thousands of Syrians crossing the borders each day, diseases already prevalent inside Syria are being transmitted to neighbouring countries, according to the WHO's regional office for the eastern Mediterranean, just days ahead of new United Nations appeals for funds to combat the humanitarian crisis. "All the risk factors that enhance the transmission of communicable diseases in emergencies are present in the current crisis in Syria and its neighbouring countries", said Jaouad Mahjour, its director for communicable diseases (n.p.).

When Nina visited classrooms in some areas in Beirut and the south-west in late 2014, she found them overloaded with children. She spoke with Oumar – an eight-year old boy living in ta camp in the south-east – who protested:

> Our camp is like a sardine can, we are on top of each other and it is very uncomfortable. There aren't enough desks and chairs so we are told to share and be fair. During the winter season, we don't have any heating means in the classroom and most times like our homes we don't even have lights because we don't have electricity.

In the same classroom was Zeinab, who according to the classroom teacher was "the outspoken girl in our class". Zeinab added to Oumar's views:

> Even though the classroom is small or maybe we are too many jammed in one class, we still have a place to go to for education. I don't mind standing up or sitting on the floor when we have extra kids in the class. Some kids only attend once or twice a week and we feel sorry for them especially Yasmeen who helps her sick mum with the washing and housework every day before she comes to school.

Life in the classrooms from a student's perspective

Initially, when Syrians fled their country as it erupted into civil war in early 2011, most of them, when they arrived in Lebanon settled in communities that shared their religious or social values. Since then, refugee numbers have been growing immensely and many have been asked to move to other areas of Lebanon. The flood of refugees is causing stress and tensions to build up between the Lebanese and Syrian communities based on the strains inflicted on society and infrastructure. To help prevent conflicts and grudges, UNHCR – working with stakeholders from both Lebanese and Syrian communities – designed what they called a Community Support Project (CPS) in 2013 and began implementing it in August 2014 in eleven communities in south Lebanon and Tripoli. The aim of CPS is to ease tensions between the host communities and Syrian refugees. The project provided daily summer activities for the children and a traditional Syrian/ Lebanese meal (a one-day event) for parents to participate in, where they could meet, socialise and strengthen inter-group relations.

Ninette Kelly is a representative for UNHCR in Lebanon and after interviewing two brothers with their families on 25th February 2015 in Abbasieh, a small town in Tyre, she said, "Since the first Syrian refugees crossed the border into Lebanon almost four years ago, Lebanese communities have extended their hospitality on a truly impressive scale" (UNHCR, 2015).

However, further complications are being introduced to the lives of Syrian refugees as time goes on. One recent worry is what to do with the bodies of loved ones when they die. And another is what about the new Syrians who are born in Lebanon? Are they now the new stateless people?

This was reported by Josh Wood (2015) following an interview with Abdul Rahim after the death of her husband due to kidney failure. She could not bury him because she was told the local cemetery was full. Luckily, her friends who lived half an hour away own a block of land and donated a small space in their land to bury her husband.

Nina asked the children and the teacher the age groups in each classroom with reference to the school levels in this, and the surrounding schools in the region. In general, most of Lebanon's public and private schools involved with Syrian refugees, did not have any issue with the children placed in an appropriate class level. Indeed, in a few cases, schools offered support outside class times to the children who were struggling, whether this was due to language difficulties or the fact that the Lebanese and Syrian national curricula teach different subjects. According to a teacher in the school in the Matn area, students' biggest challenges are in the language classes because most public schools in Syria do not teach their subjects in any language other than Arabic. In contrast, in Lebanon certain subjects such as Maths, Science, Physics and Geography are taught either in French or English.

Nina reported there were a few cases in refugee camps in the north, south-west and in Beirut where children of a mixed age group shared the same classroom because of the large number in schools and the lack of facilities and teachers. Layla, who attends a small school in the north, and Hassouni, who attends a school in a camp in Beirut, explained they have older children in their classrooms. However, they do not mind because they are very nice to them and they help them out.

Nina questioned students regarding subjects being taught in class. Most Syrian students responded by saying they were following the school subjects offered for their class level, except for the language ones. However, a few schools did provide special extra classes for the refugee children, which were organised by AVSI (Association of Volunteers in International Service) to prepare courses for Syrian children so that they could reach the same level of learning competence as the other children in their classroom. AVSI (Perini, 2013) was well aware of the importance of not slowing down the general progress of the entire class so as not to generate any hatred or blame (Perini, 2013).

AVSI has made a huge contribution to students' positive classroom experiences. For example, Amal a ten-year old young girl who goes to school in the Beirut area, told Nina she had missed out on schooling for one and a half years. If it was not for AVSI who helped her and a few other children she would have been at home cooking and cleaning, and possibly even married by now. She carried on by saying that her elder sister Dia, who turned twelve last month unfortunately had missed out on school because there was no space for her. Her parents insisted she skip school altogether and start working as a cleaner in a hospital until she found the right man who would treat her well and be able to support her and the family.

Nina discovered that most children were happy to be able to attend school, and was not surprised to learn these children did not say they didn't like school. Maybe this sentiment is a universal one. Generally, it was not difficult to arrive at the conclusion, that the students attending schools considered themselves very fortunate. Typically, the students commented:

> Hassan: "I am so lucky to have a school to attend".
>
> Jamila: "I pray every night for God to help us stay in school".
>
> Mona: "School is so very good for us and the only way to get good jobs in the future and support our families".
>
> Amal: "My father does not want me to waste time in school because we will not be able to afford the fees in few years; maybe next year I will not be able to attend, but for now I am learning as much as I can, and hopefully I can get a receptionist job and not just cleaning like all my cousins".

Nina questioned students if they considered they were missing out on education in this school in comparison to their previous school. Jamila's response was based on her particularly sad experience:

> I was very young when I left Syria and came here and can't remember much of what our school system was like, because I didn't go to school for two years, and now have been here for one and a half. I am happy now that I can catch up with what other groups are doing and no longer feel stupid.

Additionally, Nina reported how Mohsen, who works part-time on the weekends and during the evenings at a grocery shop, seemed to miss a few days of school when his employer needed an extra hand. He has very positive feelings about his school, finding it better than the previous one. This encouraged Nina to ask the students to compare their experiences in the camp schools with those back home in Syria.

Comparing school life in the camps with that back home in Syria

Nina was keen to understand from the refugee children's perspective what was different in the camp school from schools back home. Tragically, for many young children their Syrian school experiences were a dim memory. The young children in particular could not remember what the school was like back home. Moreover, many refugee children never attended schools in Syria because they were under age or the community was at war and schools were not operating. However, a few students were keen to share their thoughts with us especially. For example, Ameen explained:

> At first everything was different and it was very hard to understand what went on in the class but now two years later I am comfortable and would probably think that schools back home are different and not this one.

Nina then asked what were the similarities between the school they were attending now and their other school back home. It was clear from the answers throughout the interviews that children have some sadness about leaving their homes and schools in Syria. This sadness, however, is also accompanied with relief because they are no longer living in a war zone surrounded by fear and violence. In some areas in Lebanon, children still experience similar incidents to those from which they fled. Maha, for example, stated:

> We live in a street similar to ours back home; we hear gunshots and people fight about little things every day. The school also is similar because the teachers are always angry with us, we don't have much in the school to help us stay warm and most days no lights. This is very much like our school in Syria.

Nina asked what subjects students covered in their previous school. As mentioned above, the school system and curriculum are different in both countries. The Lebanese curriculum is structured using either the French or English language in schools to teach certain subjects such as Maths, Science, Geography, or Physics. Moreover, the use of language is certainly one of the major difficulties the Syrian children experience while in school. According to a few students, schools in Lebanon were more advanced than the Syrian curriculum. Zeina is currently enrolled in Year 5 in the Matn area. She commented that her subjects were equivalent to what she was doing when she was in Year 6 back home in Syria, in fact a year behind her Lebanon experience. Nina discovered that Zeina was not the only one to make these remarks, as other studies and reports have highlighted these points.

Supporting the curriculum in the camp schools with books and stationery

UNICEF provided stationery, books and clothing to all Syrian refugees for schooling, but according to Shaheen (2014b) writing in *The Daily Star* on a recent report by Save the Children, it was evident that difficulties had emerged in providing continuous support to refugees due to deficits and cutbacks in funding. According to the Save the Children report, many families no longer highly prioritised education, instead they used their funding support for healthcare, housing and survival (Shaheen, 2014b). Nina's observations confirmed it was obvious in some schools children received help and had books and stationery. She documented some responses from students when asked if they have their own books, pens and pencils. Jamila explained, "Oh yes, we were given all these at the beginning of the year because if we didn't my parents could not afford sending me to school and buying these as well". Mohsen had a similar answer, also adding he feels guilty because this money could have contributed towards other things for his family instead of being selfish and worrying about his education. He also said that he could not do that again next year.

"All I wish for is peace and friendship in the classroom"

At the Bekaa Valley, Nina asked the students what they would like to see in their classroom. Most refugee children said that they would like peace in every classroom and they would also like to feel safe and welcome like the locally born children. In response to the question "Do you have many friends at school?" little Alia who is in Year 4 said that she is friends with everyone in her classroom and that Madame M, her teacher, wants all the children to be friends and play together. Alia commented that the class rule is that we all share and no one should be left out.

Another question that was asked was: "Do you have to do homework after school?" Private and public schools in Lebanon started giving homework to children while they were in primary school so that students are well prepared for later years. However, Nina's experience during her visits to some camps was different, as many students did not have anything to do when they got back home. This was also reflected in the middle years and the senior years.

In response to the question "who helps you with homework at home?" it was brought to Nina's attention in some public and private schools that a few teachers dedicate extra time (an hour or two after school) to providing support for students who require help. Maha, who currently lives in Beirut told Nina that her teacher stays back and will assist four or five students every night in the library before they go home so they can keep up. She added that there are other children, who she knows from Syria, who go to other schools but do not have anyone to help them.

In some other schools there is a lively peer-support program. Some peers offer help if they live in the same area, according to Layla who lives in the north. She gave the example of Soummaya who dedicates her days to helping the teachers in the schools. Some children responded saying that their parents occasionally helped with some subjects, especially the younger children, but it became difficult when a language was involved and then the parents would have to step back. According to Abdou who lives in the Matn area, most times if the parents could not help he would not be able to do the work. A few children in the north and south-west, particularly in the camps, said their parents could not help them in any way with their homework.

Teachers, careers and other concerns

When Nina asked the children what they thought of their teacher, most respondents answered they were happy and said that they were kind and helpful. Some students reported that their teachers were moody and at times abusive and a few would not say anything. Nina interpreted this to mean they were worried about the possibility of being kicked out of school.

Nina asked 'what would you like to do when you finish school?' Bassima, who is doing Year 9 in a public school in the Matn area, had dreams about starting teaching to help re-build 'my country, Syria' and contributing towards education to ensure a better future for the next generation. On the same question, Oumar, from the south-west told Nina that he might finish school very soon and start looking for work to support his mother, since his father was still in Syria and had not contacted them for some time. He added that everyone tells him that he would not go far with education unless he was Lebanese.

The question 'What do you learn at home from your parents?' turned out to be an eye-opener that led to many different responses. Nina did not elaborate on what she was asking and left it open to the children to interpret the question through their own understanding. Moreover, children's understanding of the phrase 'learn at home' from their parents varied from one child to another. Mariam who lives in the north of Lebanon responded, saying: "I am learning a lot from my mum on how to be a good cook and keep the house clean." On the other hand, Jamila who resides in the Zahle area, interpreted the question differently and replied:

> You tend to learn all the time from your parents, you learn to talk the way they do, walk the way they do, act like them, share their interests and feelings. I look at my siblings and I can see small images of my parents. It is very funny really.

The eldest of the Salameh siblings laughed, explaining, "You learn whatever they teach you; sometimes even things that they don't want you to learn.' I asked her to give me an example and she added: 'stuff about the war and who is right and who is wrong! They think we don't know all of that already …" For Hassan, the answer was simple: "My parents always tell me that the most important thing in life is to be brave and to never give up."

Nina asked Maysoon who lives in the Bekaa Valley area about her dreams for the future. Her reply was very different to what the average twelve-year old in Australia would say:

> I don't dream often because our dreams will only add suffering to us mentally. I like to think of what I can do and am able to achieve. Fairy tales are for those that don't have anything to do and have lots of time to sit and think and I don't. I have to keep the house clean, cook and sometimes go out in the streets begging especially when we get short on money.

Maysoon also talked about her fear of failure in her life due to the lack of schooling and said:

> I wish I could go to school every day and not need to earn money to support the family. My mother can't do it all on her own. If I get work like my cousin Joumana at night I might be able to manage school as well as keep my duty to my family until my father returns from Syria.

When Nina asked Maysoon about the job her cousin holds down to bring home money at night and her age, she could not tell her what her cousin did and replied, "She does not talk about the job because 'work is work'. she says. She is twelve-years old, like me."

Like Maysoon, there are thousands of refugees in Lebanon who need an extra hand to help feed the family. Children end up deprived of schooling because they have to continuously support their families. A Save the Children report emphasises the lack of importance attached to education because it is not at the top of families' priority list. This report also pointed out avenues that children and their parents tend to rely on for survival including joining armed groups or militias, child labour and early marriage (Shaheen, 2014b). Jeffrey Dow, a Lebanese education coordinator for the International Rescue Committee, explained "according to UNHCR figures, there are over 317,000 Syrian and Palestinian refugee children from Syria aged between three and eighteen who do not have access to schools" (Save the Children Australia, 2014).

Conclusion

Social disadvantage due to lack of basic economic resources and employment opportunities of parents and carers, and trauma and loss resulting from dislocation, have been recurring themes about the situation of refugee children from Syria in Lebanese refugee camps. However, children have also displayed much resilience and coping inspite of their circumstances. One such example of coping and resilience is the ability of children to appreciate the limited learning provisions and cramped or inadequate learning spaces afforded them.

From the responses to Nina's questions, clearly, refugee children generally view schooling as important for future success. They have clear understanding that schooling will do much to ameliorate their present circumstances. But it is not an easy task, with many societal circumstances conspiring against them. Issues such as child marriages, or pressing child labour, all of which are seen as short-term answers to their pressing circumstances. Little Maysoon's home circumstances and her positive attitude towards schooling, surely, are repeated tens of thousands of times across Lebanon's refugee camps and elsewhere. The world waits with great anticipation that through the various international agencies their schooling may be improved in the sardine-can-like living conditions.

For the most part, the displaced children and their families have immediate needs to be met in order to survive. The UN, international aid agencies and the host country, Lebanon, have responded to these needs, albeit much more needs be done to address the dehumanising conditions of all refugees from Syria, especially the children. For the refugee children, employment opportunities for their parents can do a great deal for their capacity to attend schools and imagine a future for themselves, including rebuilding their home country.The refugee children's ability to imagine a better future speaks a lot about their commitment to social change.

From the perspective of the Syrian refugee children, pedagogy of the displaced suggests that educational goals should be built around raising their awareness as active participants in the world and dispel self-deprecation. The children know for a fact that they are not Lebanese and as such their access to Lebanese resources are limited, but they are citizens of the world and along with their families. They have chosen to survive in a foreign land despite seemingly insurmountable challenges. The pedagogy of the displaced encourages refugee children to speak their minds about their conditions, to question and make meanings out of their situations, and to imagine a more peaceful and safer world. The refugee children have already demonstrated this through their desire for peace and uninterrupted schooling towards a better future. Of course there are tensions, particulary in the case of the politics of hospitality, more of which will be described in the subsequent chapters.

References

Batha, E. (2013). Child marriage on rise among Syrian refugees-aid groups. *Thomson Reuters Foundation.* Retrieved 24 July 2014, from <http://www.trust.org/item/?map=child-marriage-on-rise-among-syrian-refugees-aid-groups/>.

Daou, R. (2014). Tent school offers hope to Syrian child refugees. *Yahoo News.* Retrieved 12 January 2015, from <http://news.yahoo.com/tent-school-offers-hope-syrian-child-refugees-041341979.html>.

Dingle, S. (2014). Epidemic of child marriage for Syrian girl refugees, aid agency warns. *ABC The World Today.* Retrieved 24 July 2014, from <http://www.abc.net.au/worldtoday/content/2014/s4048084.htm>.

Grant, H. & Harper, L. (2013, 29 November). Syrian refugee children face catastrophic life in exile, UN says. *The Guardian.* Retrieved 24 August 2014, from <http://www.theguardian.com/global-development/2013/nov/29/syrian-refugee-children-catastrophe-exile-un>.

Lynch, S. & Faek, R. (2014, 15 September). As the school year starts, many refugees are shut out. Retrieved 22 January 2015, from <http://www.al-fanarmedia.org/2014/09/school-year-starts-many-refugees-shut/>.

Meikle, J. (2013, 4 June). Syrian disease outbreaks "inevitable", warns WHO. *The Guardian.* Retrieved 12 January 2015, from <http://www.theguardian.com/world/2013/jun/04/syrian-disease-outbreaks-inevi table-who>.

Perini, M. (2013). Lebanon: School of Life in Marj El Khokh Camp, the Experience of AVSI, the Italian NGO. Retrieved 15 August 2014, from <http://www.oasiscenter.eu/lebanon-schoollifeinmarjelkhokh camp.html>.

Powell, A. (2014, 5 February). Perilous plight for Syrian refugees in Lebanon, child exploitation, illness among concerns cited by researchers. *Harvard Gazette.* Retrieved 16 December 2014, from <http://news.harvard.edu/gazette/story/2014/02/plight-of-syrian-refugees-in-leba non-becoming-desperate/>.

Save the Children. (2014). Tens of thousands of Syrian child refugees out of school, warns Save the Children. Retrieved 3 January 2015, from

<http://www.scaemergency.org.au/tens-of-thousands-syrian-child-refugees-out-of-school>.
Shaheen, K. (2014b, 18 September). Four out of five Syrian children in Lebanon lack schooling. Retrieved 22 November 2014, from <http://www.dailystar.com.lb/News/Lebanon-News/2014/Sep-18/271039-four-out-of-five-syrian-children-in-lebanon-lack-schooling.ashx>.
Spencer, R. (2015, 1 April). Surrendering to the camera, a four-year-old Syrian girl. *Daily Telegraph.* Retrieved 2 April 2015, from <http://www.telegraph.co.uk/news/worldnews/middleeast/syria/11508306/Surrendering-to-the-camera-a-four-year-old-Syrian-girl.html>.
United Nations High Commissioner for Refugees (UNHCR). (2001). Learning for a future: Refugee education in developing countries. Retrieved 24 July 2014, from <http://www.unhcr.org/4a1d5ba36.html>.
Wood, J. (2015, 2 March). Syrian refugees struggle to bury dead as life in Lebanon becomes permanent. *Foreign Correspondent.* Retrieved 10 March 2015, from <http://www.bbc.com/news/world-middle-east-31001100>.
Wood, P. (2015, 8 January). Winter ordeal for Syrian refugees in makeshift camps. *BBC News Middle East.* Retrieved 12 January 2015, from <http://www.bbc.com/news/world-middle-east-30725558>.

Chapter Five
Parents' Concerns Regarding Schooling

Introduction

How does the international media portray what life is like for parents in the refugee camps, and the concerns they have for their children's schooling? The discussion on this issue is described by Nina with a specific emphasis on her observations regarding parental concerns of children's provisions for schooling.

The main question that this chapter seeks to answer is: What are the parents' concerns regarding the schooling of their children in the refugee camps and elsewhere? Here we will respond to relevant sub-questions such as:

- How do parents support their children's schooling? What other provisions for schooling (i.e. non-formal education) are available to the children that their parents can give?
- How do parents address the concerns regarding their children's schooling?

Nina's initial observations

Nina felt she was very fortunate and privileged to be invited to a few homes of the refugees while conducting the interviews. She visited a number of places and viewed different ways of living and various means to make do and use what is available and most importantly what is affordable to accommodate for a family's lifestyle. The camps varied in how they were established: some were big tents made of thick fabric; others were made of tarpaulin; some of cardboard and a few were even made of billboard posters of Hollywood film stars.

The conditions were extremely poor in most tents and hazardous to all people living inside them. Nina was amazed to see people make the most of what they have and sharing their tents with an entire family – sometimes up to eight members living in the one small tent. She also visited families living in rooms built with unfinished besser blocks, and having a few gaps to let some light in. Some refugees lived in old garages and in sheds at the end of farms and in someone's free room under the house. There were those who were living in unfinished rooms on roofs of buildings and in destroyed and neglected homes left empty since the Lebanese civil war, while others resided in chicken coops and cowsheds.

Worst of all were those Nina met and spoke with who lived on the streets. These were mostly women with little toddlers in the city of Beirut, who when asked about their homes, told her that she was looking at it; they said that they could not afford to pay rent and they depended on people walking past to give a little money and hand out food. Many people appeared to be deeply depressed and traumatised from putting up with such awful conditions.

Magida's home

Nina first visited Magida's home to have a chat with her about her children's education. Magida lived in Al-Bekaa camp and hers was one of many families living there. She lost her husband before fleeing from Aleppo in Syria; he was killed while returning home from work. Now she was left to bring up her four children on her own. Magida explained she had to clean in the village nearby and do a few other chores to earn money. Her son who turned seven a few months ago was the only one who attended school. The older ones missed out on schooling for a few years.

Now Magida thinks that it is too late to send them back but the baby will go to school next year. She also said that even if she decided to send all four to school it would be impossible to afford it. The tent they lived in was very basic and it was continuously attached to many others and had hardly any furniture in it apart from the rug and a few thin mattresses on the floor given to her by the generous lady, for whom she cleaned the house and whose husband she helped in his pastry shop. Magida's young daughter, Hala, was four, followed by her son Aloush (seven years), her other son Rida (nine years) and her daughter Hoda (eleven years). The eldest two worked in the neighbourhood selling newspapers and helping in a little mini-mart most days of the week. The overall wage that all three earned between them was around $180 per month and they also received support from the United Nations with food coupons, health endorsement and funding for schooling. Magida paid about $350 per year to rent the land on which her tent was situated. She said that it was very difficult to survive and her children missed out on so much.

Magida worried much about her children's future in Lebanon. She knew that by not sending them to school they would never be able to have the money and happy life that they deserved but she could not do it: "Their education is important for sure, but feeding them and keeping them alive is more important for me", she said. Having the children help with the little income they brought in as extra for the family contributed tremendously to their survival and wellbeing. For Nina, the children seemed happy and at the time of Nina's visit they were playing outside with their friends. Magida told Nina most people in the tents near them came from the same area from back home in Syria and they often sat together and reminisced over a cup of tea on their past and their lovely homes.

Nina visits Ghazaleh from Matn

While in the Matn, Nina visited Ghazaleh who lived in a little room in the back corner on a vegetable farm, located in a very quiet area away from everything. Her room was built with besser blocks and it was approximately three by three metres wide. She was told that she was one of the lucky ones who had a room to live in. Ghazaleh was lucky because she had her husband with her. He had worked on a farm for a Lebanese family prior to the war and now had brought his wife and two boys to live with him.

Ghazaleh divided the room into three sections; a kitchen, sitting area and sleeping area. They had little cushions on the floor to sit and sleep on and a little bench to use for a kitchen. They walked for at least 500 meters to go to the toilet, which Nina could not see from the home when Ghazaleh pointed it out because it was surrounded by tall weeds. Ghazaleh told Nina that a week prior to her visit, she just missed treading on a snake that was outside her home and luckily her two-year old son was not on the tree swing that his father had made for him. Her eldest son was five and had just started attending the public school in her town. She remarked that she was not sure if she should send him; he would be better off watching his father so he could learn a trade and start helping financially at a young age. Ghazaleh was also expecting a new baby and was not happy with the situation but her words were: "it is God's will, and we can't change that".

When Nina asked Ghazaleh about her son's education and whether he liked going to school, she replied with a smile and said: "He loves going to school but when we get there he starts crying and wants me to stay. His teacher, Ms S., is a nice lady who loves looking after the children. She has been teaching for a very long time and she knows how to keep them happy but also quiet". Nina asked Ghazaleh if her son has learnt anything yet, and she replied:

> They teach them so much, I think! When we walk home every day after school he sings for me a new song that he learned and the funny part is he is learning to speak French, I don't know how I am going to be able to help him with anything at school. I can't read or write myself. My parents couldn't afford sending me to school and I got married when I was fifteen. It is going to be my husband who helps him with his home-work if we keep sending him to school. In few years, it will be tiring for him because he will have to do it after a long working day at the farm, but he will be happy to do that as he is proud that our son is able to go to school.

A family in a small village near Tripoli

Nina's third home visit was to the north of Lebanon, to a small village near Tripoli. She went there with a family friend because she insisted on going and was not allowed to go on her own because they were worried about her safety. The refugee family did not want Nina to use their names or mention the number of family members. They were happy for her to say that they were renting a small room in someone's house and sent their children to the local public school. Their living conditions were better than some others Nina had seen, and they worked long hours every day in order to simply survive financially. The mother told Nina that they were lucky because they were situated near the sea and her husband went fishing a few times a week so he could feed the family cheaply.

The house consisted of a few little pieces of old furniture that they found at the waste dump. The lady told Nina their neighbours had given them the bed as a welcome to their home. They said they received many second-hand clothes for their children, and the nice lady who lived a few houses down was a schoolteacher. She helped the children with their homework without charging the family any money.

Two of the children – both boys – went to the public school in the little village; one was in Year 3 and the other in Year 4. Their parents said that they liked going to school. However, they did not know for how long they could continue sending them to school and they hoped that if they got some education they would have a better chance to get good jobs when they were older. The parents hoped that maybe when they went back to Syria the children would continue their schooling there. To Nina, they seemed happy with the school and spoke positively of the teachers. Their biggest fear was that if the children reached a certain year in their education in Lebanon, the government would prevent them from doing so. Furthermore, the ability to carry on with education due to financial strains or lack of places in schools posed another concern.

Ms X in Beirut

The fourth and last home Nina visited, was situated in Beirut and it was based on a few remnants of rooms in an old hotel that had been destroyed, but never rebuilt when the civil war ended. It was a total mess, and Nina could not hide her amazement about their living conditions when she walked into the place. She confessed she was at a loss to know how the children survived the poverty, lack of hygiene and safety in that place.

Both parents told Nina they were blessed to have children who were strong and had a great immune system. Their children stopped going to school for a few reasons: first, the schools did not have places to take all of them; and secondly, the parents were struggling financially to keep them in school. They needed the children to start help bringing in some money to the home. They still had one small child, who was probably three years of age and clung to the mother the entire time Nina was there. They told Nina that a few people who they believed to be from UNESCO or UNICEF, had visited the a short while ago. Apparently, they wanted to talk to them about the importance of sending their children to school to give them a chance to live a normal life.

Ms X was very upset with these organisations and bitter about their approach, particularly when they criticised what she and her husband are trying to do. She added, "No one can love our children more than us, what do they know about normal life? How can these kids be normal after what they have seen and been through? We are doing the best we can and at least we kept them alive. I think we know better what is good for our kids and their future".

On the streets of Al-Hamra in Beirut

All other interviews took place in public schools and in non-formal schools, on the streets of Beirut, in small villages and on a few occasions where these children were actually working. For Nina, this situation was starkly different.

Nina stopped and asked a lady who was breastfeeding while begging on the streets of Al-Hamra in Beirut on 28 September 2014 if she was hungry, and offered to buy her and her three children sitting by her side something to eat. She looked at Nina with amazement and wished her good health and prosperity, saying that it would be very nice to feed her starving children. Nina went to the shop around the corner and came back with some food. She had a few tears on her face and all she had around her were a few plastic bags. Nina handed her the food and stood there and asked her name and if she sat on the same spot every day.

She said that Nina could call her Mariam, and she started telling her that she lived on the streets and she moved from time-to-time to the busiest spot so she could attract people's attention and get food and clothes for her children. It was a hot day and they were sweating while sitting down with her.

Mariam would have been in her late 20s but you could see the world's miseries and injustice in her sad eyes. She said that she came to Beirut when she was pregnant but her husband was still in Syria and had not yet seen his baby. Her husband could not get out because he had to look after his old and frail parents. The youngest boy she was breastfeeding was eleven months old and the daughter was three years old. The eldest son was five years old. Nina asked Mariam if she would like to send her eldest to school one day and she shook her head and looked at her strangely as if she was making fun of her. Mariam remarked:

> I need help to support them all, he might need to help me begging soon so we can feed all of them until my husband comes and joins us one day. What would schooling do for us? It would not provide us with bread or milk.

Mr H and the visit to a school in the Matn area

Nina visited the school in the Matn area one afternoon around pick-up time, as suggested to her by one of the school administrators. She was told that this would be the best time for her to get to speak to parents. Nina sat outside the classroom on the bench in the primary school and started a conversation with a middle-aged man sitting next to her. After a brief introduction, Nina asked him if he came from Syria and where is he living now. The man – Mr H – was very reticent and did not have much to say at the start until he realised that Nina was not a local and came from Australia. He then straight away turned towards her and said that they once owned their own small business up until a few years ago.

Some parents in Aleppo

It was a sweet shop in Aleppo and he was certain that it was no longer standing. He added that he and his wife used to bake and prepare everything. They used to export their sweets to the Gulf to places such as the United Arab Emirates, Kuwait and Bahrain and also to Sydney, Australia. With a sad smile on his face, he looked at Nina and said, “We were doing very well”.

A few parents who Nina spoke to remarked they were not fortunate to continue their education beyond Baccalaureat. A few mothers said they got married prior to completing it and others did not have the finance to keep them going so they found jobs in offices and shops. A gentleman called Abu Nader told us that he was a mechanical engineer and worked for the water company in Syria. Mr Hassan told Nina he worked as a nurse in Dar-Al-Shifa Hospital in Aleppo for seven years prior to the war. In contrast, Ahlam who was a schoolteacher in Syria prior to her 'dramatic shift', as she called it, said that she was luckier than other women in her situation because she could still make use of her teaching by continuing to help in the non-formal school where her children attend in the Bekaa Valley.

With reference to parents' thoughts and beliefs about the schooling their child/ren received, Nina encountered different attitudes depending on the area and the school that children attended. In general parents were very pleased and grateful that their offspring got to go to school and they were impressed with the government's generosity for not charging them any school fees. Some negative comments from parents in relation to schools were received:

> The school can take the young child but not the one that goes to middle school. They told us the classes are full; what do they expect us to do?
>
> Schools should run some special classes for our children. The kids struggle to follow the Lebanese curriculum especially having to deal with the French language. No one seems to be able to help and we both can't speak the language.
>
> This would be a temporary fix for the children and one day they will not be able to do anything with their education because they are not Lebanese (Haifa, commenting on her children who went to an PRS school in a camp in Beirut.

Nina also asked people about what sort of education they thought their children were receiving. Again, the majority of parents we spoke to were very happy with the education that their children did receive. The few who had criticisms to voice were: firstly, those who did not get in because they were not registered; and secondly, whose children already attended non-formal schools.

Parents' plans for their children's future and the importance that education played

During the interviews, Nina asked most parents about their plans for their children's future and the importance that education played. Many parents were very concerned about the future but did not seem to hear the word 'education'. Some of the responses were as follows: "The future? What future do we or our children have?" This was what Ahlam had to say shaking her head in disgust. When Mariam was asked the same question, she commented that her children would grow up as refugees in a country away from the people they grew up with and loved. She also said that her children would probably not see their grandparents anymore and even their father, who could not escape from Syria. She regretted that the only future she could see was a sad and miserable one for them.

On the other hand, there were a few parents who seemed to have heard the word 'education' and not just the word 'future', and Mr W. told Nina that if refugees kept receiving help and support in education it would be excellent. If it stopped, however, then most parents would have had to cease sending their children to school because survival matters came first. Another parent, who was slightly more comfortable financially and sent her children to a private school in the Matn area, explained to Nina, '"Nothing is more important than having a certificate in your hands, I keep telling my children, you can always land on your feet no matter what. We hope that we can provide for them that privilege, since we cannot give them anything else".

Parents' views about their children's teachers; their support for their children

Many parents talked about the positive attitude that teachers did show to the children and the care and support they provided for them, which was enormous. Most of them were happy with their teacher's approach to the children's sensitivities due to the extremely traumatic situations that they had been through. For instance, Um Saleh told Nina that her children were so blessed to have the teachers they had. Some parents, however, had different views about the attention their children received in school and commented that some teachers tended to favour the Lebanese children and offered them more help and support.

Ms L. said to Nina that her son had to ask a question at least three times before the teacher paid him any attention, but if it was a local child he/she received an answer almost immediately. This was made clear in more than one interview with certain parents who commented:

> Some teachers have a problem with our kids because they cause them more work and I can understand that but it is not fair for our children to notice that tension and feel guilty all the time because if we had a choice we would have been in our homes and schools back in Syria.

Nina asked the parents if they encouraged their children to read and write at home and found this question to be a little tricky. Half the parents were keen to support and push their children with their studies while others did not seem worried about it. A lady from the Beirut area said, "They can do what they are capable of, and we will not be pushing them around. They have suffered and seen enough." Furthermore, another parent from the Bekaa declared, "Encourage my children maybe, but more than that will not work." Mr A. smiled and asserted, "who cares if they did not go to school at all. They are at least alive."

The answers Nina received can only reflect the suffering that these people had to bear and continue to bear. Survival was the only important thing they focused on at this stage of their lives.

Many interviewees said that they spent a reasonable amount of time helping their children with their homework but not with the language aspect of it. One Syrian-Palestinian father said that he could help the younger ones, but his eldest son, Ahmed, tended to have work beyond his educational capabilities. A few mothers said that they were able to help especially with the Arabic subjects. Nina was keen to hear the parents' responses when she asked them if they thought that their children received enough education. The responses varied according to school and region, but in general most parents were happy that there was some form of education available. There were those who were positive and their comments were as follows:

> We are very pleased with the school and the teachers are very kind and merciful towards our children.

> My daughter is getting more education than she received in the last war years. She can only remember war and suffering.
>
> Our children are learning a lot and it is impressive to hear them speak to us in French at home. They are not fluent by any means but they tend to show off in front of us (Mr Salameh).

Although a few parents were less positive, they still responded by showing happiness that their children did receive some education:

> As long as they are learning to read and write for the time being and not in the streets learning how to hold guns and fight, we are happy.
>
> Attending and learning a little is better than not knowing how to hold a pen or read and write, we will encourage them as long as possible.

However, some parents did resent those teachers who were biased against their children and responded to this situation by saying:

> They are learning very little in the camp and are not interested. What can I do? They don't get the same attention that other Palestinian children do.
>
> Our kids know that they are not wanted in the classroom and that is why they don't want to learn.

On the question of receiving financial aid for schooling material such as books, stationery, etc., all registered refugees stated that they received help and support from UNHCR in Lebanon and from other countries such as Iraq, Jordan and Turkey. The generous support offered by the Lebanese Ministry of Education (MoE) in 2012 opened many doors and opportunities for Syrian refugees. The MoE requested all the country's schools to waive school enrolment fees and provide all students with free study materials. Other education programs supported the refugees with funding such as the Jusoor Refugees Education Program, which is a private support group formed by Syrian expatriates. The ex-United Kingdom Prime Minister Gordon Brown requested that $500m should be provided for Syrian refugees' access to education in Lebanon, according to Nouha Ghosn, President of WILPF Lebanon (Ghosn, 2013). Other charities have also helped Syrian refugees, such as Caritas, a Roman Catholic charity, and Save the Children which conducted after-school classes to help prepare Syrian students to enter Lebanese public schools (Cochran, 2014).

With reference to the question concerning what parents taught their child/ren at home, most parents referred this question to the school curriculum at first, until Nina explained to them about informal education and asked what would they like their children to learn from them. She received a variety of reactions and open-ended responses. Most parents wanted their children to understand what happened in Syria and how the war started, and they wanted them to stay away from the temptations of violence and crime. One respondent told Nina he hoped that his children would not experience a war but he still wanted to teach them how to be resilient in case this situation arose one day. For example, Mona's mother said, "I want to teach my children to love and forgive but I don't want them to be victims and naïve at the same time". Other parents wanted to prepare their children for the future because they see it as a bloody one ahead, especially for the next few years. One parent, who wanted to remain anonymous stated, "I want to be logical about the situation and if we were asked to leave Lebanon one day I want my son to be ready to defend himself."

Nina also asked parents if their child/ren liked to go to school every day. For Nina, it was surprising to have many parents confirm their children did look forward to attending school on a daily basis. There were, however, a few who said that they needed their children to skip going every now and then to help out with a few jobs around the place:

> As soon as Hassouni hears a little sound in the house he gets up and starts getting ready. I think he likes to catch up with the children at school.
>
> Mona hates the snow because it stops her from attending school even when she says to us that she was so cold in class during the day she still wants to go.
>
> Our daughter Yasmeen wants to be a doctor she says and help all the injured people (Yasmeen's mother).
>
> I wish I could allow my daughter to go every day but I need her help with the baby and the house sometimes; I am getting weaker (Oumar's mother).

Parental strategies for maintaining a focus on their children's schooling

Nina asked how parents motivated their child/ren to remain focused on their schooling. It was interesting to receive a variety of responses to this question and the extreme points of view that parents had, ranging from those who strongly supported and encouraged education to those who found that it was out of reach and not very useful. A majority of parents told her that they would stand behind their children and remind them of the importance of continuing their education in order to live a better life. Conversely, a minority said that they had no intention of sending their children to school, and even encouraged them to search for work instead. They complained that the education system was not Syrian and that since their children had already lost a year or two it would be useless for them to start all over again. A few parents also were worried about the safety of their children at school and therefore did not want to send them to be educated in places that were far away.

Mr and Mrs Salameh told their children that they were happy for them to work as long as the children went to school and one day returned the favour by having a degree and starting a good job that would bring pride and money to the family. Soumaya, the volunteer helper in one classroom, said that she talked to the children and told them that having an education is what might save their country and allow them to return to Syria one day. In the Bekaa Valley camp a single mother told Nina: "Education is not the answer to survival especially when we can't have enough to eat. I can't lie to my children and motivate them when I am not capable of keeping them alive." Finally, another parent who lived in the Beirut camp informed Nina, "Motivating our kids to survive is our priority before education. "

Conclusion

Recurring themes from the perspectives of parents on the schooling of refugee children from Syria included survival, social disadvantage, justifying child labour, parental helplessness and self-deprecation, need for continued financial support from external sources, importance of school certificate for future employment and significance of learning about peace and forgiveness.

For most Syrian refugee parents it is evident that their children's survival is their over-riding priority – health and welfare come first before schooling. But then, when they do feel secure, generally parents recognised the importance of schooling for the children. Many parents are managing the means to facilitate their children's schooling because they recognise the importance of the certificate for getting a job and getting ahead in life. Many Syrian parents of refugee children, while recognising that their children will receive some formal education from their peers, parents and society, believe that it is formal schooling which counts in life. For them schooling is everything, as many parents commented to Nina.

Nina's research shows that parents are proactive in searching out state and community assistance for their children's schooling. Sure, conditions are far from perfect at home, with many pressures on parents encouraging them to take short-term choices to avoid schooling their children. However, many parents adopt the long-term view and do everything possible to get their children to school. Many children look forward to what schools provide.

How do the Syrian parents' perspectives inform the pedagody of the displaced?

Parents' involvement in their children's education and schooling is important. They communicate both positive and negative advantages of schooling to their children. Always there were the underpinning tensions due to the politics of hospitality. Refugee parents driven by the most basic need to survive often rely on their children to help support the family's survival. When parents unintentionally teach their children helplessness, self-deprecation and lack of present and future opportunites, children are at risk of demotivation in attending school. This perpetuates a vicious cycle of lack of schooling leading to even more limited economic opportunities for children. Education begins at home. As significant adults of children, parental support of their children's education can make a huge difference. Charitable institutions and relief agencies both local and international can help refugee parents to make ends meet through provision of basic amenities, financial support, and much needed employment opportunities.

References

Cochran, J. (2014). The education of Syrian refugee children. Retrieved 11 January 2015, from <http://www.mei.edu/content/at/education-syrian-refugee-children>.

Ghosn, N. (2013). Lebanon's burden: The crushing consequences of Syria's refugee crisis. *Women's International League for Peace and Freedom.* Retrieved 20 December 2014, from <www.wilpfinternational.org/Lebanons-burden-the-crushing-consequences-of-syrias-refu gees--crisis/org.com>.

Chapter Six
Teachers' Perspectives and Challenges

Introduction

What is life like for teachers in the Syrian refugee camps in Lebanon? This chapter begins with a consideration of the some of the literature that has been written on the subject, and then a description by Nina of her general observations regarding teachers. This chapter addresses the main question:

What are the teachers' perspectives on schooling in refugee camps in Lebanon? Moreover, the chapter attempts to answer the following relevant sub-questions:

- What is taught in the schools for refugee children in Lebanon?
- What curriculum is followed?
- What resources are available to teachers?
- What challenges do teachers encounter in their teaching?
- How do the teachers respond to these challenges?

Types of Lebanese schools

There are various types of schooling in Lebanon, and it should be emphasised here that originally there were four different types of schooling prior to Syrians seeking refugee there, with the subsequent establishment of NGO schools, UNICEF and the informal schools. These four original types of schooling were:

- **State schools**: These schools were run by the MoEHE and school fees began at $47 per annum in primary schools and cost $80 a year, for secondary schools. The fund is used to pay for wages and deal with unforeseen damage to schools' infrastructure. The Saudi Arabian government funded all Lebanon's state schools and covered the registration fees and textbooks for all the students enrolled (Hamdan, 2013).
- **Free-private schools**: In reality these schools are not "free" because the fees cost parents approximately $533 per annum. There are 363 free-private schools in Lebanon and are subsidised by the MoEHE. Religious groups manage three-quarters of these schools, while the remainder are run by NGOs or are owned by private individuals (Hamdan, 2013).
- **Private schools**: These schools have the highest number of children attending education in Lebanon. There are 572 private schools in the country with tuition fees ranging from $1500 to $15,000 per child per year (Hamdan, 2013).

- **UNRWA**: These schools are available in the twelve Palestinian camps in the country for all registered Palestinians. There are 74 of them and recently there were 32,059 children enrolled in them, a similar number to those attending private schools. UNRWA schools are totally free of charge and the students receive free stationery and textbooks (Hamdan, 2013).

Teacher registration

Concerning the current state of teacher education in Lebanon, having a university degree, plus the completion of teaching courses at the Lebanese University are necessary prior to registration with the teacher registration board. Previously a teaching diploma, as well as a university degree, was the standard (Hamdan, 2013). A private school teacher could register in the Teachers' Syndicate. Alternatively, a public school teacher had to be registered with the Lebanon Teachers' League (Hamdan, 2013).

Post-civil war schooling in Lebanon

During the severe disruptions caused by the Lebanese civil war, between fights and battles, some schools could still open their doors for students. In some areas such as Beirut, schools were totally destroyed and many children were denied education for years. Nevertheless, some families were fortunate enough and owned or rented homes in semi-safe areas outside the battlefield zones to which they moved out of the city during the war. Other families migrated overseas to live better and safer lives. Many schools served purposes other than just education during the civil war; some were shelters for those who lost their homes or functioned as hospitals. Despite all the horror, bloodshed and fighting, many schools when possible insisted they carry on with teaching to distract the children, educate them and guide them towards a peaceful future. In some areas the principals were desperate for teaching staff because not everyone would risk their own life and safety to travel to certain villages to get a teaching job.

Such fear and instability opened a few doors to volunteers who were keen to teach and help the children, but "they were not fully qualified to participate in the education system," said a Deputy School Principal, Ms Georgette. Currently, some schools still employ a few teachers who are not fully qualified and are not members of the Lebanon Teachers' League, according to Mr A. who worked as a school principal until 2013 and is now retired. He told Nina:

> In private schools it is slightly different because they have different policies to the ones in public schools, which are totally controlled by the MoEHE (follow all their policies and seek permission for accreditation). Some schools would employ people who don't have teaching qualifications but they might have maths or science degrees. Other schools would employ graduates with psychology degrees to help the children who were once traumatised and lost family members or homes amongst other things.

Mr A. stopped talking for few minutes, looked up towards the sky, took a deep breath and continued at length:

> I lost so much during the war but I could not let others miss out because I was suffering. I lost my wife and three children who lived in the South area while I took the job that I was doing at the time but they wanted to join me. My wife told me that her life and the kid's lives are not more precious than mine and that they were coming to live with me. They were safe in the South and I did not want them to take any risks but their time must have been up as a bomb hit them while travelling. I stopped working for seven months after the tragedy. My life stopped totally. You can say I gave up. A dear friend of mine approached me and begged me to get back to work and assist children who need help to prevent more deaths, violence and blood. He made me realise that I was being selfish and self-centred and could do much more by helping in schools which got me going back to work.

Mr A. told Nina that he employed a few teachers who were not members of the Lebanon Teachers' League but they had very humanitarian qualifications:

> I offered places in schools for good people who wanted to promote peace and stability – not just those who are qualified and only want to teach a subject. I wanted teachers to teach how to be human, how to love, how to forgive, how to live together in harmony, I urged them to spread different messages to children and their parents, messages of being compassionate and standing up against those who want to fight,

standing up against violence and disagreements in religions. I was not the only person who had enough of the tragic situation and the years of violence and war. The majority of Lebanese have had enough. We wanted all this to stop.

Similar views were voiced by most interviewees – parents, teachers, children and community members. They wanted the violence to end, but the requirement for teachers being registered or otherwise varied from public to private schools and formal to non-formal. This was particularly the case in recent years when the MoEHE again took full charge of its teachers. This was an account related to Nina by Mr Wael from the Matn area.

A deputy principal in the Zahle area, Ms Georgette, also told Nina that a few teachers did not renew their registration for many years while the country was in turmoil, due to financial hardship, apart from the closure of most departments' doors. She also remarked, "Qualification and registration alone are not sufficient for good education in Lebanon. We need all teachers to promote acceptance, understanding and respect between the many religious and political groups that live in this vastly diverse country".

"Were you a teacher prior to this position?"

Most teachers working in their profession in Lebanon are qualified and they must register with the Lebanon Teachers' League. The MoEHE implements policies and manages compliance along with the Public Elementary and Secondary Schools' Teachers League, the Teachers' Syndicate and the Educational Centre for Research and Development (ESDP) (SABER Country Report, 2010). A few volunteers are also able in more recent times to offer their time and support to help in schools, especially with reading and mathematics sessions in primary classes. This is due to the increase in the number of students since the Syrian refugee crisis began. These volunteers tend to support children who are a little behind in their skills, and their confidence and self-esteem are worked on. A public school principal in the Matn area, Mr Wael, told Nina his school would be penalised heavily if it employed a non-registered teacher.

Apart from the few Syrian qualified teachers in their country and who volunteer to work in some schools, all Lebanese teachers were registered. On the other hand, in the Bekaa Valley it is a completely different story. There were in fact a few teachers in the camp who had no teaching qualifications, but they were very bright, articulate and supportive of the children. Here, Ms Hala explained, "in the camps in particular there are some amazing teachers that bring back lost smiles to the faces of the children". She continued:

> Teaching is not only about learning how to read the alphabet and know how to add 1+1, teaching is to provide life skills for the children; it is about survival especially in our situation in Lebanon. We have just got out of a civil war and now trying to support the Syrian refugees with their depression and understanding while their country is at war. This is very difficult for the Lebanese, Syrian and Syrian-Palestinian Refugee (PRS) children.

Teachers are not only worried about the extent of their subjects and duties; they wanted to provide all manner of support to the children. It was clear to Nina, as Ms Bouchra in the Bekaa Valley remarked on the public schools, that children did not have access to a counsellor for support. A teacher had to provide such support as well as manage a classroom and teach her/his subjects every day. This was far from easy to do with children who were traumatised, mentally scarred from war and everyday violence, and lived in an environment where families suffered financially, mentally and physically.

The curriculum and subjects taught to Syrian refugee children

With reference to the subjects being taught, the majority of teachers taught subjects they were qualified in, those who completed a maths degree taught mathematics, while those with geography taught geography, and so on. Similar to the education system in Australia, many teachers tended to teach extra subjects and not just their major or specialisation. However, it was slightly different in the camps. When Nina visited them, she observed in certain situations that some personnel were appointed as teachers with no formal qualifications, but still provided support to the children and general education especially with literacy and numeracy.

Nina wanted to know if teaching complied with the Lebanese National Curriculum. On 15th November 2014, the Ministry of Education and Higher Education (MoEHE) announced while schools were still accepting Syrian students in the morning programs, they would also create more options for enrolments by allowing students to attend schools in the afternoon. This decision agreed with that of the UNHCR and UNICEF, organisations committed to supporting 57,000 Syrian children during afternoon classroom lessons in public schools (UNHCR, 2014d). This announcement came as a relief to many teachers in schools because it reduced the student numbers in class on one hand, but on the other hand, teachers such as Ms Georgette, Ms Bouchra, Mr Wael and Mrs Imm Rami explained, "lower number of students but longer teaching hours daily".

Conditions in the classrooms

Most Lebanese public schools in 2012 opened their doors to Syrian refugees as instructed by the then Minister of Education, Mr Diab, and later in 2014, schools introduced the afternoon classes for Syrian children. These catered for a large number of refugees without overcrowding the classrooms; in recent times the Lebanese newspaper *The Daily Star* obtained a memo sent internally to schools in October 2014 from the Minister of Education, Elias Bou Saab, informing them to register only returning refugees or their siblings to school. This deprived newcomers aiming to start school in 2014 of the opportunity to receive an education (Shaheen, 2014a). The announcement clashed with the one mentioned previously by the Minister of Education and forced many local communities to open small educational institutions in addition to the informal UNICEF funded schools to cater for children in surrounding villages; the survival of such institutions depended on the support of volunteers.

There has been an increase in volunteer private tuition in Syrian refugees' tents, run by people who cannot obtain employment in Lebanon, but would like to help educate the Syrian children. During Nina's visit to one of the camps in the Bekaa Valley, Mr Aswad told her that he had dedicated three hours a day for nearly eight children in his camp to come with their pens and papers, between 11 am and 2 pm every day, for what he called the "love of knowledge". He added that at the beginning most children were hesitant, but now they arrive before lessons start because they enjoy learning from him. Mr Aswad was not a schoolteacher in Syria, but his qualifications as a civil engineer allowed him to teach the children some maths and how to read and write.

All teachers interviewed by Nina seemed satisfied with how much their schools did to provide the maximum amount of support and education for local children and refugees. Ms Hala was certainly not embarrassed to show off when speaking to Nina over a cup of coffee about the efforts they had put into welcoming and comforting all their children. The number of students in classes outside the camps was no longer as overwhelming as it was before the introduction of the double shift in schools (one morning shift and one afternoon mostly for Syrian refugee children to keep up with the high numbers) said Ms Bouchra, especially not having to "jam" children of all age groups into the one classroom. She mentioned that at some stage she had students varying in age between eight to sixteen years, remarking that this situation intimidated many children and embarrassed many others as they all felt out of place. However, in recent weeks with the extra support the classes became more organised and welcoming. Ms Bouchra added, "Since I teach the 4th Year, most children in my class vary in age between eight and nine years, this gives me the opportunity to put all my energy into their education and well-being."

In the Beirut area, Ms Hala informed Nina that in their camp they did not have enough classes to support all age groups and therefore they were forced to have children between the ages of six and ten in the same classroom: "This certainly makes it hard on the teacher as well as the students but at least we have them in schools and we try to make it fun to all."

Regarding whether Lebanese classrooms are all full, it must first be stated that the country's school system can cater for 300,000 students. However, it is now the case that out of a total of 1.2 million Syrian refugees, half of which are children under the age of 18 according to a recent UNHCR report – 930,000 are of primary school age, but only 270,000 are registered with UNHCR in Lebanon (UNHCR, 2014a). Mrs Imm Rami who works in a public school in the Matn area, considered, in fact, conditions were much worse. "The schools were full and overcrowded, teachers and children suffered equally from the lack of space, teaching material, teachers' capabilities to cope with the large number in class and children not receiving the attention they deserve." However, recently and thankfully due to the piloted programme that took place in 2013–2014 in the town of Arsal in the north-east of Lebanon, an afternoon shift for refugee students has been supported by the MoEHE and UNHCR. It was implemented in 74 Lebanese schools and catered for over 27,000 Syrian refugee children throughout the country (UNHCR, 2014a).

Mrs Imm Rami told Nina that in her small primary school which is located in a village in the Matn area, the total number of children enrolled is 129, fifty per cent are Syrian and the other fifty per cent are Lebanese. She added:

> All refugee children are very good at school, especially with the Arabic subjects because their strength is mainly in Arabic. They pay more attention than their Lebanese peers in class because as we know that most Lebanese parents who send their kids to a public school in Lebanon are those who don't put much value on education and many try to avoid paying the fees charged. However, by saying that, I am generalising and have to say that there are some families that have no choice but send their kids to public schools because they can't afford the financial strains with having to come up with large sums for private school fees. Syrians refugees need only to pay for the reception year level but not for primary or secondary because they are free of charge for all Syrians as MoE requested.

Syrian children continue to miss out

On the question regarding the dropout rate, the organisation Save the Children recently reported four out of five Syrian children in Lebanon do not attend school (Save the Children, 2014). Additionally, the dropout rate of Lebanese children attending public and semi-private schools is very high for a nation that places a high emphasis on education (Hamdan, 2013, p. 13). These dropout rates are the consequence of: first, students failing a year and not wanting to go back and repeat it; secondly, the low standard of education; thirdly, the punishment regime that is still carried out for misbehaving in most schools even after it was made illegal; and fourthly, parents' decision to withdraw their child or children on the assumption that schooling is wasteful and poverty plays a major role in making such decisions (Hamdan, 2013, p. 12).

The aforementioned Mr Wael commented at length on the topic of Syrian children missing out on schooling:

> In state schools the drop-out rate is very high, people get fed up with the lack of facilities and the poor conditions in schools, but most times when a student fails the academic year this means having to repeat the same Year, which also means more funding strains on the family. This is when they make a decision to withdrawing the child by saying they are not made for schooling and they should go out to the workforce.

In contrast to the Hamdan report, Mrs Imm Rami from the Matn area talked about the dropout rate specifically in relation to the refugee children in her school. She asserted that the dropout rate was virtually non-existent. Ms Bouchra, who worked at a primary school in Bekaa Valley, emphasised the fact that refugee children rarely stop education while they are still in primary school. However, the dropout rate tended to start when they reached the age of eleven or twelve years, as reported by UNICEF (2013a). This is most likely the result of regulation changes made in 2004 by the MoEHE allowing students to move from one Year to another no matter what results they achieved for at least the first three years of their education. It was envisaged this would reduce the dropout rate in schools and keep them in schools for a little longer (Hamdan, 2013, p. 3).

When asked about her opinion on this decision to allow students to progress, no matter what grades they received, Ms Georgette declared:

> This is only a band-aid solution to the problem, the first few years of a child are the foundation of their schooling and if the foundation is not strong enough the whole plans will collapse. In my opinion, we should deal with the matter in a different way instead of pushing the kids to discomfort which totally means a drop-out when they are no longer getting the automatic climb in grading.

Lebanese parents' views and a very special school

When parents were questioned regarding this change in regulations, most of them seemed excited about the idea and said this will keep their children in schools longer; they did not have to pay for the same year level twice. Nevertheless, some Lebanese parents expressed their disappointment with having to pay for their children's education while the Syrian refugees were perceived as receiving their children's education for free. Ms Hala informed Nina there were often complaints to the school principal from local families about having to pay for their children, while others did not. She said that being through a civil war in Lebanon prior to having the Syrian refugees arrive made it much more difficult to justify how such decisions were made. At least the Lebanese were still in their own country and lived in their homes.

Shaheen (2014a) recently reported an interview with Mr Alloush, a Syrian mechanical engineer refugee who is currently teaching maths in one of the informal schools. The school for Syrian refugee children is known as Beyond Schools. He said that "they are trying to break the routine of education" by introducing teaching in the form of songs. Beyond Schools hires teachers from Lebanon and Syria to create harmony by improving the interaction of Lebanese people and Syrian refugees and reducing unemployment for teachers in Lebanon (Shaheen, 2014a).

Destroyed schools and generations of children

Lebanon's public schools receive funding from the Ministry of Education and other organisations (UNHCR, 2013a) to support the refugees. All fees are waived for Syrian children who are in primary schools, but this is not the case for secondary or kindergarten institutions. However, having to teach the extra afternoon classes in public schools did not mean that teachers were paid for that. According to one school principal, Mr A., most teachers worked five to six hours a day in a class with students where the average class size varied between 25–30 students in some schools.

Miss Assi is the executive director of Beyond Association, a UNICEF-funded organisation. She is a Lebanese NGO representative who operates informal tent schools in the Bekaa Valley, and was quoted as saying: "If you see a destroyed building you rebuild it, but if you see a generation of children destroyed, what are you going to do?" (Shaheen, 2014a). This is basically the situation that teachers faced in schools where it was their responsibility to promote positivity and happiness in order to rebuild this generation of children. The world that was destroyed as mentioned by Miss Assi reflects on most refugee children that we came across and talked to; they all seemed so sad, lost and their hopes and dreams were shattered.

Ms Georgette showed Nina some of the work her Year 4 class produced when they were asked to draw pictures or write a story about their dreams. Unfortunately, photos of their work could not be taken, because the teachers felt uncomfortable. Nina promised to respect their privacy and confidentiality. Many of the pictures the children drew included their "dream homes", equipped with big showers, large kitchens, big gardens, and lots of furniture (mostly beds and bunk beds). A very interesting feature that appeared in most homes was having bars on the windows, which reflected their fears and insecurity.

It was also very pertinent that not even one child in her class drew or mentioned toys in their picture. One child sketched a picture of an aeroplane with himself and his entire family on it including his uncle and aunt who died in the war. On the other hand, one fascinating girl wrote a story about her dream of freeing the world from bad people who go around killing everyone. A slim, tall young boy wanted to build a big tank that targeted the bad people and killed them all, while a few others had ideas about amusement parks and travel opportunities for sad children. Ms Georgette was correct in saying that these children did not live a normal life due to their displacement. She was also proved right by saying that they were still children who deserved to have dreams and should have been living freely and carelessly.

Most teachers and principals Nina spoke with, emphasised the importance of providing for these children the maximum amount of comfort and normality in schools while they were away from their homes, and having to hear or see things that reminded them of why they had fled their homes and sought refuge in Lebanon. When Nina spoke to the school principal Mr A. in the south-west of Lebanon, asking if the increase in students affected in anyway the behaviour in school in general, he smiled and replied:

> Children are children worldwide. They tend to react to situations that they live in. If you live in a house with depressed parents you will become depressed; if you live with violent parents you will become violent. We have to remember that leaving your home and living in a place that you don't want to be is not an easy thing to tolerate every day. Most families have lost family members, friends, homes, they feel 'undignified' as one mother said to me in our school, and it is not easy for them.

Similar to what Mr A. told Nina was the reply of a school coordinator in the Zahle area, Mrs M., who expressed her concern about children skipping school because of the availability of child labour in certain areas of the country. Ms Bouchra also touched on this problem, adding she hears other teachers speak of children disappearing especially during the harvest season. All teachers interviewed commented about how children's behaviour was influenced by the areas in which they lived and the locality of their schools. They also mentioned the attendance of children – whether Lebanese, Syrian or Syrian-Palestinian – varies from school to school based on the area that the school is situated in and on social class.

Conclusion

The Lebanese and Syrian teachers' perspectives inform the pedagogy of the displaced through the themes on social empowerment, free education, promotion of social values (peace, harmony, acceptance, diversity, respect and understanding), volunteerism, compassionate education, restoring human dignity, confidence-building and addressing trauma and loss. Schools and teachers are undoubtedly the cultural brokers of schooling and education for liberation.

Clearly, the teachers looking after the needs of Syrian refugee children in their schools are in their unqualified commitment similar to other teachers, the authors have observed in other countries. We can only remind ourselves of Nina's fellow Lebanese Australian, Joseph Wakim (2013) who in the preface to this book, called for an international perspective on the unfolding tragedy of schooling or the lack of it in Lebanon's Syrian refugee camps.

The Lebanese government's response to the crisis has been positive, and obviously much appreciated by the Syrian refugee community. Yet, hundreds of thousands of children continue to miss out on the universally acclaimed right for an education. This is but one manifestation of the politics of hospitality. Part of the solution to this is to provide more schools and train more teachers, and hence, continuous funding of education.

References

Hamdan, H. (2013). Education in Lebanon: War Child Holland. Retrieved 24 January 2015, from <www.warchildholland.org>.

SABER Country Report. (2010). Lebanon teachers. *World Bank.* Retrieved 29 January 2015, from <http://www.wbgfiles.worldbank.org>.

Shaheen, K. (2014a, 27 October). Schooling for Syrian refugee children gets inventive. *The Daily Star.* Retrieved 10 January 2015, from <www.dailystar.com.lb>.

United Nations High Commissioner for Refugees (UNHCR). (2014d). Second shift schools offer hope to young Syrians. Retrieved 26 January 2015, from <www.unhcr.org/530b65326.html>.

United Nations High Commissioner for Refugees (UNHCR). (2014a). 2014 Syria regional response plan: Education. *Vulnerability Assessment for Syrian Refugees (VASyR), WFP, UNHCR, UNICEF.* Retrieved 14 July 2015, from <http://www.unhcr.org/syriarrp6/midyear/index.html>.

United Nations High Commissioner for Refugees (UNHCR). (2013a). The challenge of education: The future of Syria refugee children in crisis. Retrieved 20 September 2014, from <http://www.unhcr.org/syria/the-challenge-of-education>.

Chapter Seven
Community Concerns and Responses

Introduction

What is the nature and extent of community concerns for Syrians' schooling inside and outside of the Lebanese refugee camps? What does the community do in regard to the schooling and education of children? How does the community find the available support for these children's education? How does the community respond to challenges in terms of the children's schooling? Nina visited many locations to investigate and record her observations of community leaders in the camps and in schools providing for Syrian and Syrian-Palestinian refugees. Her observations are triangulated against secondary sources.

Before visiting the camps, Nina commented she kept reading about the very few temporary/informal tents built for the Syrian refugees to live in, until the situation settles in their country and they were able to return to their homes. It was made clear the Lebanese government refused to build permanent camps and would penalise anyone who does build them. She approached her fieldwork with much trepidation.

Available resources in the camps

Despite the articles that Nina has read about the official rejection of creating permanent camps, she was shocked when she arrived in the Bekaa Valley and saw fields of never-ending tents. They were all situated in little clusters only a few kilometres apart. She saw children running through the streets, eating in the street, and playing soccer in the middle of busy main roads between cars. It felt like a bad dream in which children were out of control and no one could save them.

During Nina's travel to the Bekaa Valley, only a few family friends who had a sound knowledge of the area and which roads to take well, accompanied her, for safety reasons. When they arrived at one camp Khaled, a family member in the car knew the guard who was sitting on an old iron chair, with a large machine gun and a few grenades attached to his belt. Khaled handed him a few Australian dollars and informed him of a scheduled appointment previously organised with a schoolteacher at the camp.

The guard was very pleasant, opened the gate, which consisted of a few barbed wire rods pulled from one side of the road and connected to a hook on the other side. He smiled, as he felt important, apparently for being in charge of making decisions, pointed out the tent and waved goodbye.

As soon as the car drove in the camp, children started popping up from everywhere. They started running after the car and screaming with loud voices, "talk to me, I will tell you what you need to know, please". They had their hands out also as if they were begging. It was the middle of the week, around midday in mid-October and none of these children was obviously at a school.

Mr Fadel and Ms Hanaa

Before reaching Mr Fadel's tent – the man who Nina was intending to interview – from the distance between the voices of the children and the dust blowing around in the sandy camp, her attention was caught by the shadow of a man waving, trying to catch her attention. The children got to him before Nina. As soon as the car parked and everyone got out of the car, a very warm welcome was given to all and a quick invitation by Mr Fadel to Nina. He smiled and exclaimed, "Welcome to my humble tent" as he called it, and added "this will help us get away from the curious harmless children".

Everyone walked into the "humble" but very tired-looking tent. His wife was there to greet Nina and her companions. She was holding an infant in her arms. She said "hello" in English and uttered a few other words that did not make sense to Nina.

Nina told them that she can communicate well in Arabic and that there is no need to try and speak in English. Ayah, the wife of Mr Fadel, was very happy to hear that and explained to Nina straight away that she can only say a few useless words in English that she learnt in Syria while watching TV. She was very thin and short and had a very pale but pleasant face.

Mr Fadel waved his arm around the place and said, "this is our humble little tent that gives us shelter and privacy – and pointing out to the pot belly in the middle of the room – this year we are hoping for a warmer winter after almost freezing to death last year". The tent was very basic; it had a large carpet that covered the dirt floor with cushions to sit on and a small wooden coffee table. They used the oven in the potbelly fireplace for roasts and baking cakes, but Ayah informed Nina that she uses the cooker outside mostly in the summer to save money and save the tent getting hot. A small plastic vase with artificial flowers placed on the floor in the corner between the cushions added a little bit of colour and life to the place.

Mr Fadel was a schoolteacher in Syria prior to his asylum to Lebanon. He said that he taught "Hisab" (Maths) for fifteen years to secondary school children. The children outside the tent kept calling and asking Mr Fadel if they could come in and speak to his guests. Looking to Mr Fadel, Nina said that they were yelling out, "Sir, are we allowed to speak to them?"

He replied they get many journalists and volunteers asking questions about the refugees' lives in the camps and in the schools. He went on to tell Nina that since he settled in this area he decided that he must do something useful for the Syrian children whose parents could not afford to send them to school. Therefore, he set up his own little class after speaking to the parents in his camp and they all agreed to send him the children for a few hours each day for some education. Mr Fadel explained he teaches around twelve children for three hours a day for five days a week. His focus is on getting them to know the basics of reading and writing. He does this voluntarily because he wants to help them to get some form of education and also because it gives him something to do. Mr Fadel went on to explain he was concerned about the future of his newborn daughter, Alia, and her education.

Like Mr Fadel, Ms Hanaa – a Syrian refugee dance teacher – is now running voluntary dancing sessions in the Zahle area for all interested Syrian refugee children. Nina went to see her after hearing from a student attending the Zahle public school about the fun time that children have on Sunday while dancing. Her so-called studio was a neglected public property, located in an empty shell of a house, which was destroyed during the civil war. This house was situated at the end of a side street behind a local rubbish dump. Hanaa was proud of her studio and the fact that she can engage and amuse children to help restructure their days and fill it with fun activities rather than reflections on the war, sadness and fear they have recently faced. Hanaa mentioned that dancing keeps her fit and her mind occupied and her wish is to have more children join because more of them means more laughter and fun that they can have and share.

The demand for schooling in the camps

The UNHCR reported in September 2013 that the number of registered school-aged Syrian children with UNHCR was 270,000. Within a few months it was expected to exceed the number of Lebanese children in schools, bearing in mind that there are still around eight per cent of refugee children not attending schools (UNHCR, 2013e). The incursion of the large number in schools is changing and affecting the quality of education available to both locals and refugees (UNHCR, 2013e).

A revealing article by Hussein Dakroub (2013) published in *The Daily Star* and titled "Education and services bolster coexistence in Tibnin" highlighted the important role that education played in keeping a little Lebanese southern country town called Tibnin stable and a model for good relations between Muslims and Christians during the civil war. Mr Fawwaz told *The Daily Star,* the large number of educated people in the little village that is located about fifteen kilometres from the Israeli border, with a majority of Muslims and a minority (approximately 10%) of Catholics, is what saved the town from the sectarian tensions in the country. He explained: "Education is a special feature of Tibnin. The town has graduated a large number of Army officers, teachers, judges as well as MPs, ministers, including the current Parliament Speaker" (Dakroub, 2013, p. 3).

Amazingly, under the same article in Dakroub (2013) on the same page there were two other articles. The first one was titled "Recently arrived Syrians face hardship enrolling in school", in which Mr Fares reported that he had been trying to enrol his eight-year old son in a school at Deir Zannoun. He was told that he had no chance because there were no vacant places. He said that he contacted the NGO Save the Children as well as public schools in surrounding areas and spoke to a few school principals. The response was negative, as he was told no more places were available for Syrian refugees.

The second article titled "Sidon schools overwhelmed by number of refugees" written by Mohammed Zaatari (2014) articulated the struggle in the refugee camps of Ain-El-Helwi and Mieh-Mieh. The twenty schools that already accommodate the 10,000 local Palestinian students were now overwhelmed by the arrival of the new 3,600 Syrian-Palestinian families, as well as the 330 Syrian families to the Sidon area. Local schools with the assistance of URNWA were trying to help 2,700 Syrian-Palestinian students in finding places and be distributed in the three camps in Ain-El-Helwi. Meanwhile, the Syrian families could live in the camps, but the Syrian students were not accepted in schools run by URNWA.

This contradiction between the report referring to education as the reason behind peace and stability in the small country town and the other two that follows saying that there is no room in schools for refugees seeking education or only room for Palestinian-Syrian children and not Syrian refugees, made us realise that it will be a long time before education reaches everyone. Not having enough facilities, rooms, teachers, financial support and having to house and educate a devastating number of children does not facilitate the provision of equality in education to all.

Some personal responses

While in the Bekaa Valley, Nina spoke to a few members of the Lebanese community, asking their opinion on having camps appearing in the area and how the situation affected their daily lives. Most people were sympathetic with the circumstances especially when they could see the hardship and condition that the refugees were in. Mr B., a business owner in the area, said it was important to remain human about what was going on around them and to support people as much as possible. However, he also pointed out that Lebanon had, itself, been through so much and he hoped that the refugees were not planning on fighting their war and demanding their rights from Lebanon. His wife who was by his side agreed with him, adding forcing those children to have an education was the only way to divert peoples' minds from war and aim for some kind of stability.

Zahle was not much different; most interviewees wanted peace for everyone and wished that the war would end in Syria and that the refugees could return home. Ms Heyam, a volunteer who helps in the hospital in the Zahle area and has a son who goes to the local school with Syrian children, said that there was always the fear that the situation would escalate because many people thrive on fighting and this is how they get financial aid. "The worry to most Lebanese would be that the refugees bring with them the war from Syria into Lebanon. The numbers are rising alarmingly", Zahle explained, "and we have to remember that Lebanon is a very small country that is still trying to get out of the financial problems as well as many other issues since the civil war ended".

Ms Heyam held Nina's hand and confirmed to her that this does not mean at all that children or their parents need to suffer or be denied a safe place for refuge and aid. Unfortunately, the politicians must be careful and be aware of such risks and the precedent it could set. She also mentioned that the Syrian lady who lived a few houses away from her, with her three children, was crying all the time because her husband and four other children, had been trying to cross the Lebanese border for over six months and were repeatedly rejected. She feared she would never see them again; apparently, there are new rules requiring complex documentation if one wants to cross the border.

According to Amnesty International Australia, (2014) Syrian-Palestinian refugees from Syria seeking shelter in Lebanon, Jordan and Turkey are facing restrictions and are being asked to provide more complex documentation. Yet, they are mostly denied entry. Evidently, some sources leaked information to Amnesty International Australia informing them that regardless of what documentation the Syrian-Palestinian refugees provide, they would not be allowed to enter Lebanon by land or through the airport (Amnesty International Australia, 2014) in the future.

In the Matn area there were a few individuals who voiced their worries and concerns as well, by saying that their scars had not healed yet from the violence and terror that the Syrian army put them through in the late 1970s and early 1980s. However, they felt that lending a helping hand to victims like the majority of the refugees is the least that our community can do. Imm Rami told Nina that in her little village most people empathise with the refugees and they help by offering them clothes, food and job opportunities when they have functions such as weddings and funerals. These at least present themselves as opportunities to make money.

In the north near Tripoli, it seems that the communities are immersed in helping the refugees in many ways like the other little villages with food supplies, clothing and house needs, according to Ridah when she spoke to Nina. Ridah also told Nina the families seeking shelter in Lebanon are ones who want to forget all about the troubles and start a new life with their children away from sadness and death.

Warda, the refugee lady who was living in a room on the ground floor in the same building as Ridah, was keen to speak to Nina. She hoped that her message could be spread beyond Tripoli and Lebanon. She wanted the world to know that people are not all the same; they are victims to political stands that leaders are taking, but in which innocent people end up as the victims of war. Warda lost her husband when a bomb exploded near him in her town in Syria. Her son, Kamel, who has just recently turned eight was with him. "Mercifully" she said, "he only lost his eyesight". Many more heartbreaking stories were shared with Nina. Millions of people lost so much from family members, to homes, to land, to body parts, to dignity. The list goes on.

Beirut and its community

Beirut and its community were not much different, since it is a busy and crowded city. However, tensions here were milder because Syrian people are mixed in with many others who suffered during the Lebanese civil war and are battling poverty and depression. When asking a few Syrians in the camp about their experience of the support they are receiving from the wider community, most were thankful for being offered opportunities to get rooms to stay in. The responses Nina received from interviewees in the Lebanese community were along the lines that "we must help people when in need. We have been there and we know what it is like". This is what Mr A. said while sitting in the little coffee shop having his Shisha and playing backgammon with his friend Mr H. Mrs H. told Nina with embarrassment that people from her community are pressuring her and her fifteen-year old son to go back and fight in Syria so they can make some money to survive and live in a place on their own instead of having to share a room with three other families. It was made clear to Nina that there were twelve people living in one room because they could not afford to pay any rent.

Refugees also seemed to be sharing homes and burdens in the south of Lebanon inside and outside the camps. Places were crowded with refugees and the conditions of most places Nina visited were appalling.

Halima was an interviewee who shared a house with a family of six who she had never met prior to she and her family moving in with them. She wanted to speak to Nina but kept looking sideways as if someone was threatening her. She said that she has so many stories to tell about the situation that her family and many other refugees are in. All her stories were distressing, she talked about her two sons, Mahmood and Hassan, who were both under the age of thirteen, but were working to support themselves and the family.

Halima also had two daughters, Julia and Ola, who were aged two and six respectively, but she was frightened to send them to school. Her husband became very ill and died only a few months ago so her children will be growing up fatherless. She was grateful to the community for providing jobs for the boys. Her boys would have loved to go to school but that would have meant starvation for the family. Many families she said had to rely on food vouchers and aid from the UN and charity from the locals but that was not enough. Halima told Nina that her children would have no hope in having an opportunity to establish a good life for themselves and all those dreams that she and her husband had for the family were shattered the minute he got sick. Halima's elder daughter was holding a little doll that she dressed up in a black rag and was pretending to put her to sleep. Halima was one of many who has lost every ounce of hope.

Community effort in regard to the schooling and education of children

What the communities actually did regarding schooling and education, was confusing and complex and difficult to generalize about, as they depend on each community's social eminence, geographical location and its political status. Throughout Nina's journey and her visits to the camps it was evident that many communities outside and inside the camps provide general support to Syrian refugees, be it clothing, medicine, food, means for heating such as gasoline, blankets and much more.

In the Matn area Mrs Imm Rami told Nina that the school library was constantly used for teaching a group of Syrian refugees because this was the only room available to run classes in. As mentioned earlier, there are indications at times that Lebanese people are fearful that this will be a replay of 1948 and the rise of the Palestinians' camps in Lebanon that were only meant to be a temporary solution at the time. However, these tent camps have now transformed into fixed concrete homes; the Syrians themselves fear that they may never be able to return to their homes and the families they left behind. All three peoples – Lebanese, Palestinians and Syrians – have experienced enough deaths, violence and war, which makes it hard to expect them to just move on and forget what they have been through.

A report in *The Guardian* (Brown, 2014) drew attention to a small village called Akroum situated in the north-east part of Lebanon bordering with Syria, where a few Syrian teachers worked jointly with local teachers and the community in the village. They were allowed to share the school for a few hours each day to provide education to the Syrian children in the afternoons after the Lebanese children had gone home.

The community finding available support for the children's education

Since the number of Syrian refugees coming into Lebanon has increased and the public schools are overflowing with children even after the introduction of the afternoon shift to most public schools, which allowed an extra 75,000 to 90,000 children to enrol, there is still a desperate need for more education centres such as the stopgap centres currently providing some form of education to those who are not fortunate enough to have room in a school.

Located in a small refugee camp in the Bekaa Valley, Bar Elias is one of the many education centres that hosts 220 children. Jusoor and SAWA for development and aid are both education centres funded by NGOs and they provide schooling to unfortunate children who were left out due to the lack of vacancies. These two groups as well as UNHCR, which operates its own education system, known as Accelerated Learning Programs (ALC), are a few out of 20 that provide education support in Lebanon for Syrian and Palestinian-Syrian refugee children. The setback that these educational centres regularly face is that they often run out of funding and halfway throughout the academic year they are forced to shut down (Rosenthal, 2014).

The problem with such an education system according to Ms Bouchra is that these centres have no official standing. Students will not have proper documentation of proof for their education in such centres and therefore there is no guarantee for a place for them when applying later in formal schools. According to her, many schools do not find these centres to be sufficient sources of knowledge. One parent, Mr. A., on the other hand, praised the centres for doing such marvellous work by allowing the children to stay in the system and giving some, who missed out on at least three years of education, a sense of strength and hope.

Community response to challenges of schooling refugee children

UNICEF recently developed a new strategy called "No Lost Generation" which intends to provide access to quality education and protection for all refugees and the host communities (UNHCR, 2013e). The strategy faced many challenges, such as children dropping out of schools, treatments in schools, cost, place, availability, transport, curriculum, disability, discrimination, bullying and violence. During the interviews for this book, 'socialising and sharing thoughts about education' as Nina called it, it was revealed that many people – in fact, almost sixty per cent of participants from all areas involved in this study – when asked about their children's schooling, said that they were not going to school or sent only a few children to school while others were sent to work. This means that a very disturbingly large number of children are missing out on education. The challenges people in the community emphasised varied in importance and reasoning, but mostly all related back to affordability and safety. People in most communities thought that it would be very important to educate all children to stop an entire generation from becoming illiterate.

Nina interviewed a community member in Zahle, the focus being on the long-term effect on children who missed school. The reply was that reality is harsh sometimes and depressed and displaced people tend to have different priorities to what is known as a normal lifestyle. Mr Fadel in the Bekaa Valley shared similar thoughts and added that what may seem to be important for some people may be trivial to others. He emphasised he knows education is not a trivial matter, but when it is compared to survival it becomes a lesser priority in life.

Maha explained that maybe certain communities should force children to go to school to prevent violence and promote safety to all. She also mentioned in some towns due to violence and distraction some young refugees have been locked up at night with the cooperation of their parents as requested by the community to save their lives and the lives of others around them. According to Maha, if those young people get some education to redirect their thoughts and imaginations the violence might diminish.

In the Shatila camp in Beirut, Nina spoke to Umm Ahmad who suggested she would be the first person to ensure her son stayed in school and feed him knowledge if she could be guaranteed that this brought peace to her home country and they could return to their villages. However, the reality of all this is was that if Ahmad did not work and bring home money they would not be able to survive.

"There are many individuals in the community who offer help to refugees in many forms. Some would donate furniture, clothing, food or offer some little jobs here and there", explained Imm Rami in the Matn. In general the community would like to see the refugees comfortable and self-sufficient, but it might be a long time before this happens because according to her Lebanon is very expensive in comparison to Syria. Life is more demanding especially when people have lost everything and they have to start again from scratch.

Different views emerged on many political issues within most communities in Beirut, Zahle, the Matn, south of Lebanon, in the north and the Bekaa Valley especially with reference to the support or lack of it concerning the Syrian government. This is why Nina emphasised her main concern and topic of discussion would entirely focus on the impact of education in the refugee communities. There were those who believed that education is the answer to a better future while there were others who prioritised logic and reality to ensure survival.

More community support and action for the children's schooling in the camps

After a long and steady discussion – especially with parents in the community whose children are attending schools, it was obvious to Nina most parents were excited their children were getting some form of education. When Nina asked them what more they would like to see the community do to support their children there were a few suggestions concerning transport to school. A few parents stressed the difficulty they faced with transport, stating that it was very expensive and costs parents around $70 for the bus per annum. Umm Ahmad said to Nina, "We can"t afford that money, school is so far for the children to walk, my children suffered enough in Syria and I don't want to put them through that again. What would I do if something happened to them when they are at school? How can I get to them to bring them back home? I can't risk sending them anywhere".

Mr Fadel explained to Nina that many parents have children who are traumatised and some are also handicapped and have been injured during the war. Parents would like community support in the form of medical services to help reduce some children's anxiety and to provide medical assistance to many who have health problems. He described one child in his camp who was badly burnt before escaping to Lebanon and he said that the boy does not leave his tent because other children look at him strangely and he feels as if he is scary to all of them. Mr Fadel elucidated the fact many children are scarred mentally more than physically and need extreme attention and help. Ms Bouchra mentioned that one of the problems faced in public schools was the lack of counselling support. She said such help did not exist in public schools and to have private sessions was very expensive. She also explained most teachers lack the experience of dealing with children who have experienced war. After many years of battles and bloodshed during the Lebanese civil war, one might think that the government would automatically include such training while preparing teachers for their career.

Another challenge mentioned by most people with reference to schools and expectations was the language barriers confronting Syrian children. Syrian parents were seeking help from individuals in the community to provide support for their young ones to excel in schools. This issue was backed up in a few communities already where interviewees mentioned to Nina that their children had been receiving help from community members. Ms Bouchra assigned a few students in her school tasks to help the newcomers – as she called the Syrian children – so as to help them adjust to the school and its system. Also many parents in a few communities such as Zahle, the south (Batroon and Koura), and the Bekaa Valley mentioned to Nina that they continue to extend a helping hand whenever possible to the students in need.

The northern regions of Lebanon introduced a new project known as "Strengthening Education for Vulnerable Syrian and Lebanese Children in Northern Lebanon", which provides Lebanese and Syrian refugee children with an opportunity to get back to school and catch up with their education. The project is operating in public schools and in community centres to offer assistance to students struggling with the Lebanese curriculum and in particular the language component. This project works side-by-side with the ALP (Accelerated Learning Programs) to facilitate the hurdles for those children who have been away from education for a while but are willing to return. They also provide tailored workshops for parents and guardians to assist in child protection and dealing with war-traumatised children. A good example of this is the organisation War Child's "Strengthening Education for Vulnerable Syrian and Lebanese Children in Northern Lebanon" (War Child Holland, 2016).

A recent study conducted by One Hope and Near East Initiative (OHNEI) focused on religion and spirituality and its effect on Syrian refugees in four regions in Lebanon (OHNEI, 2013). When this topic was mentioned many refugees spoke highly of refugee humanitarian work that was sponsored by the Christian churches and Islamic mosques equally.

In Zahle, Mr A. informed Nina that his family would always be grateful to the support they received through the church. It was the moral support and caring that kept the family going, he added. Mr Fadel also reinforced this statement when he told Nina "when life gets tough, we look up to the sky and speak to God". He also explained although a Muslim means that he must pray five times a day, this is something he did not do. It does not make God love him any less, he thought, as long as he was praying and that should be enough. Mr A. said the mosque in Beirut provided shelter and food for many Syrians, especially receiving warm clothing for "our children which was such a blessing".

"Lebanon street-based children report" is a new study carried out by international organisations under the direction of UNICEF (2015), which looked at 700 children from Syrian and Lebanese backgrounds who do not attend school but are forced to work. The study revealed the majority of children worked between four-sixteen hours a day, earning a minimum of $3 to a maximum of $12 hours per day when employed at a car repair garage, in a coffee shop, at a supermarket or selling tissues and chewing gum in the street. The highest paying wage was for prostitution and that reached $36 per day. The heartbreaking results reported in this research study generated a pledge by the Lebanese government to eradicate abusive child labor by 2016. However, due to the current political situation in the country and previous experiences with exploitation laws, this pledge is virtually pointless (Shaheen, 2014a).

People in the Lebanese community showed their concern with jobs caused by the readily available cheap labour coming in from Syria. Mr H. said that when employing a Lebanese person there would be some etiquette and expectations of your fellow countryman, but employing a Syrian person did not require going through any formalities, and the cost would be much cheaper; often less than a third of the price. He informed Nina that many of his family members and friends employed young Syrian children in their mini-market, in the coffee shops and as mechanics because they comply with all requirements without any complaint and he was aware that they would be physically abused when they did not perform accordingly.

One Lebanese mother, Mrs Hanan, living in the north part of the country, looked after children suffering malnutrition and lacking good sanitary conditions, by offering them food and clean clothing. She suggested to Nina children are stronger at defying hunger, but struggle when it comes to sexual abuse and exploitation. Supporting the issues raised in the article on child brides already mentioned in this book, Hanan mentioned a few stories about families in her neighbourhood saving the honour and lives of their daughters by marrying them at the ages of thirteen and fourteen. Hanan explained that living expenses, schooling and medical services put many families in situations where they had to make decisions beyond their will.

Conclusion

The schooling resources of the Lebanese school communities clearly are stretched to their limits due to the massive influx of refugees from Syria. In communities which have in their recent past already experienced the terrible disruptions through their own civil war, many individuals suffer, and many school-aged children suffer terribly. Most countries around the world recognise that an investment in public education is one of the smartest investments they can make in the long-term interests of its community members. They recognise that crime in its many guises and other insidious elements that can erode society will be overcome when its citizens are adequately educated. The sheer pressure which the Syrian refugees bring to Lebanon's school communities means that they only provide support for primary school-aged students, and local school communities have very limited resources. School communities are left to provide for pre-school aged children and secondary school students. While Nina observed many examples of wonderful community responses to the needs imposed by the rush of Syrian refugees in respect to school education, she did not need to look far to find suffering and vulnerable children.

The perspectives of members of the refugee communities (Syrian and PRS) and the host Lebanese communities inform the pedagody of the displaced through themes on encouraging provision and accreditation of non-formal education, volunteerism, harnessing the expertise of some members of the refugee community (teachers, engineers and other professionals), collaborative action among Lebanese and Syrian communities, addressing xenophobia and stereotyping, empathy, provision of employment opportunity, provision of logistical support (shelter, transport, medical and psychological/counselling). Despite the reality that opportunities in the communities (refugee or Lebeanese) are not equal and often hard to come by, members of community do come together in the spirit of peace and tolerance. Some challenges are addressed while many others are works-in-progess.

References

Amnesty International Australia. (2014, 1 July). Families torn apart as Palestinian refugees from Syria denied entry to Lebanon. Retrieved 19 February 2015, from <http://www.amnesty.org.au/news/comments/34938/>.

Brown, G. (2014, 24 January). A brilliant scheme for making sure Syria's child refugees get and education. *The Guardian*. Retrieved 15 January

2015, from <http://www.theguardian.com/commentisfree/2014/jan/24/syria-child-refugees-school-education/>.

Dakroub, H. (2013, 14 September). Education and services bolster coexistence in Tibnin. *The Daily Star Lebanon*. Retrieved 24 January 2015, from <http://www.dailystar.com.lb/News/Lebanon-News/2013/Sep-14/231232-education-and-services-bolster-coexistence-in-tibnin.ashx>.

Hamdan, H. (2013). Education in Lebanon. *War Child Holland*. Retrieved 24 January 2015, from <www.warchildholland.org>.

One Hope and Near East Initiative (OHNEI). (2013). Children in crisis. Retrieved 10 February 2015, from <http://onehope.net/wp-content/uploads/2014/04/Children-in-Crisis.pdf>.

Rosenthal, M. (2014). Lebanon aid groups scramble to build schools for Syrian refugee children. *The Huffington Post*. Retrieved 12 March 2014, from <http://www.huffingtonpost.com/2014/02/26/syrian-refugees-schools_n_4855751.html>.

Shaheen, K. (2014a, 27 October). Schooling for Syrian refugee children gets inventive. *The Daily Star*. Retrieved 10 January 2015, from <www.dailystar.com.lb>.

United Nations High Commissioner for Refugees (UNHCR). (2013e). The challenge of education: The future of Syria refugee children in crisis. Retrieved 20 September 2014, from <http://www.unhcr.org/syria/the-challenge-of-education>.

United Nations International Children's Emergency Fund (UNICEF). (2015). Lebanon street-based children report. *#ChildrenofSyria*. Retrieved 15 July 2015, from <http://childrenofsyria.info/2015/02/16/lebanon-street-based-children-report-2015–2/>.

War Child Holland. (2016). Strengthening education for vulnerable Syrian and Lebanese children in Northern Lebanon. *War Child*. Retrieved 20 September 2014, from <http://www.warchildholland.org/project/strengthening-education-vulnerable-syrian-and-lebanese-children-northern-lebanon>.

Zaatari, M. (2013, 14 September). Sidon schools overwhelmed by number of refugees. *The Daily Star Lebanon*. Retrieved 24 January 2015, from <http://www.dailystar.com.lb/News/Lebanon-News/2013/Sep-14/231234-sidon-schools-overwhelmed-by-number-of-refugees.ashx>.

Chapter Eight
The State and Policy Support

Introduction

Since the beginning of the Syrian crisis in 2011, Lebanon has been home to 1.5 million Syrian and Palestinian-Syrian refugees, according to the United Nations High Commissioner for Refugees (UNHCR, 2014b). This influx of Syrians has put great pressure on the local Lebanese community in terms of the efforts to provide food, health services, education and employment. The overwhelmingly high number of refugees is exacerbating the political and economic pressures that Lebanon is still experiencing due to its own civil war (International Labour Organization, 2014).

This chapter provides insights into the support that the Lebanese state provides as host to the refugees in terms of schooling for refugee children. Moreover, this chapter reflects on the following question: how does the Lebanese state respond to the issue of schooling of children in refugee camps?

The Lebanese government response and challenges

Lebanon's Ministry of Education has permitted refugee children to enrol in public schools and has organised morning classes and extra afternoon shifts so that these children can get as many opportunities to education as possible. Despite the facilitation of this path for refugee children there are nonetheless significant impediments such as discrimination, transportation, cost of education and cost of living that prevent such an opportunity as being worthwhile in the long-term. A major problem is that the school systems in Syria and Lebanon have very different curriculum structures and mode of language.

As measures of control, the MoEHE announced that for Syrian refugee students to be enrolled in Years 9 or 12 – Brevet or Baccalaureate – they need to provide documentation proving they qualify to enrol in these Years. This is what Ms Georgette, a school principal, told Nina. If students cannot provide the official paperwork required to confirm their eligibility to enrol, then they have no chance of enrolment. When Syrian families have crossed the Lebanese border illegally this means they are not registered, which could be due to their fear of being reported to the authorities in Syria. Refugee families are scared they will be punished one day when they return or their remaining family in Syria could be reprimanded or worse. Consequently, being unregistered means that these students cannot sit the Lebanese official school exams.

The one solution for this problem as suggested by the MoEHE would be for parents to contact the Syrian embassy and request the documentation required for their children's schooling. Due to their fear of reprisals meted out by the Syrian regime, most unregistered families are not prepared to do that, especially if they still have family members residing in Syria (Addis, 2013).

A humane response

Mr Wael told Nina that like himself, some school principals have offered optional local exams for Syrian students to assess their compatibility with those undertaking the same Year in Lebanon. If their performance was equivalent to their Lebanese peers, then they were offered a place in the school. The unfortunate aspect of this enrolment is that it will only permit them access to the school without being eligible to sit the final official exams. Mr Wael also talked about the choice some parents make for their children, which is to have them enrolled in a lower Year to facilitate their educational path without requesting the requisite paperwork from Syria.

Another recent study by UNHCR (2014b) indicated that Syrian refugees experience many challenges while in schools and these include violence, hostility, discrimination and lack of educational support. This development forced MoEHE to request support from UN agencies in the form of help to deliver afternoon classes that are exclusively customised for Syrian children and their curriculum. An interview conducted with the director of Amel Association, Dr Mohanna, who works closely with NGOs and INGOs to support health and education for the Syrians refugees' security, stressed his concerns about their safety and wellbeing. He pointed out the worsening situation in their country and how the political situation would affect stability in Lebanon because one side of the political party supports the Syrian regime and the other opposes it (Migration Policy Centre, 2014).

The organisation World Vision helps close to 150,000 refugees by giving them food vouchers, access to clean water and hygiene kits. It also offers supplementary classes to children in schools and helps find places for those who are not yet enrolled as well as what they call the Child Friendly Spaces to provide psychological support to children. These spaces help children to overcome their emotional wounds by participating in fun activities (Addis, 2013). During Nina's visit to the south and north of Lebanon, a few interviewees mentioned to her the financial aid from World Vision with particular reference to food vouchers. Mrs Hanaa told Nina that she was blessed to have her son work with Jamil who owns the local grocery shop in their neighbourhood and how he used to give her time to pay her bills until the next food vouchers arrived.

The tragedy of housing pressure and crises at home in Lebanon

According to Mrs Hana's story as told to Nina, it seems that most refugees living in the north are living with relatives, or in some situations living with other refugees to whom they are not related and have not met before. Most refugees living in the Bekaa Valley, either were placed in tents, or rented properties and shared with others to minimise costs. Alia, the girl from the Matn area, mentioned earlier in this book, whispered into Nina's ear the fact that so many houses in the Bekaa Valley are unfinished, but added, "Sadly, they cost an arm and a leg to rent and most people are struggling to survive, therefore, you find that up to twenty people share a one-bedroom apartment". It is a similar situation in the south and in Beirut with of course the extremely tragic cases where people live on the streets, under bridges or under tree shelters (interview with Mariam, 26 September 2014) and reduced to being virtually beggars. Both the Lebanese community and the state, contend with this dire predicament of the refugees in Lebanon.

In January 2015 Pierre Prier, journalist for *Al-Araby Al-Jadeed English*, a Middle East news and current affairs organisation, conducted an interview with the mayor – Mr Daher – of a little village called Karoun. This village has a population of 5,000 people and it is situated in the Bekaa Valley. The mayor stated he cannot accept more than 5,000 refugees in the village because such a huge increase in its population will deeply compromise its viability and security. Karoun hosts about 120 tents, divided into two separate camp sites to keep it practical, and Mr Daher emphasised the point that he will not allow permanent fixtures to be built. He also added that there are rules and measures put in place that refugees must follow, even though many think that this is a means of controlling people. Yet, if they are willing to stay in his village they must register, report and have their details checked to receive aid until the situation improves in Syria (Prier, 2015). According to Mr Daher, each city and village in Lebanon will benefit from following a similar procedure to best deal with the large number of refugees seeking shelter.

Education status of Syrian refugees

A study done by the International Labour Organization (2014) drew attention to the low enrolment rate of the Syrian refugees. In general one out of three is illiterate, and only a third of the population has attained primary education and barely 3% has reached university level. In comparison to the eighty-one per cent enrolment rate for Lebanese children in pre-schools, the Syrian children's enrolment rate is a very low three per cent. While it seems more comforting for primary education reaching five per cent it drops again to nineteen per cent for secondary education.

These figures reflected different explanations for the dropouts such as geographically-based schools where the Lebanese enrolment rates are normally lower than average in areas like Tripoli and Bekaa Valley. The higher age group of children at primary level (aged between eleven and thirteen years) is due to repetition of school years, children not being registered, and parents not finding it safe to send their children to school. The most common reason was lack of finance (ILO, 2014). An important point to make was that the report did not find the number of working children significant. This was documented to be eight per cent while the early marriage of girls was at the rate of five per cent. This situation contradicted the situation that emerged in Nina's interviews, which showed that almost every family she spoke to having children over the age of nine, had at least one working member providing the family with financial support.

With the aim of getting 400,000 out-of-school refugee children into education institutions in Lebanon, UNICEF and the Norwegian Refugee Council implemented non-formal education projects sponsored with funding from the UK's Department for International Development (DFID). It focused on five particular regions in Lebanon and the essential health needs such as water, sanitation and child safety (Rainey, 2014). A family living in one of the regions in the south explained to Nina how such a project saved the futures of her eight children.

Mr and Mrs Hasan reflected on their frustration at not being able to pay for their children's schooling prior to sending them to one of the non-formal schools in their area. Mrs Hasan explained to Nina that by sending her children to school she not only saved their future but also saved their family from creating enemies because the children were getting very bored sitting all day at home and they were noisy and mischievous. According to her, six of her children are very happy attending the program, but the older two are not able to go because they missed out on a few years of schooling and they need to work.

The non-formal program includes all sorts of activities as well as having an educational benefit. "The program introduced sports for the children and a supportive program for us parents, guiding us on how to protect our children, the benefits of sending them to school, how to prevent violence in the home and gives information on other issues", said Mrs Hasan. Nina was told a few other anecdotal stories by other families in which they all shared their appreciation for the Lebanese state that allowed such programs to be delivered. They were also very thankful to UNICEF for its support.

The town of Arsal in the mountains in north-east Lebanon has witnessed the addition of 80,000 people to its original population of 60,000 since the civil war in Syria began. Most refugees who sheltered in Arsal come from the Syrian city of Homs, and they found residence in a wedding hall and a mosque and were provided with blankets, food packages, kitchenware and soap by the UNHCR. The Bekaa Valley provided shelter in the form of camps and rented rooms for over 400,000 refugees (UNHCR, 2015a).

Many attempts have been made in Lebanon to encourage refugee children to attend schools. Lebanon has provided teachers, the extra afternoon shift, the funding provided for enrolment and education stationeries and books as well as transport and assistance with language and curriculum. However, a press release from the conference organised in Amman by the Centre for Lebanese Studies, UNHCR, UNICEF and UNESCO on 25th June 2014 announced that fifty-three per cent of Syrian refugee children were still not attending schools. The conference explored many options to deal with issues facing public school systems as well as key issues associated with curricular strategies for effective learning for both refugees and host communities and certification (Centre for Lebanese Studies, 2014).

The Lebanese government policy has implications for the provision of education to Syrian refugees. Under the international network for education in emergencies (INEE) law and policy formulation, free and inclusive access to a safe schooling environment is clearly stated (Shuayb, Makkouk & Tuttunji, 2014, p. 39). Consequently, refugees have access to formal and non-formal education with some modifications to formal education in terms of the curriculum, merging the language of registration in which refugees can register in Syria but attend schools in Lebanon, and availability of the Libyan curriculum and a Lebanese-Syrian combined curriculum. Some schools in the private system have introduced the Syrian national curriculum, which was not recognised by the Lebanese government. The government later introduced special classes only for Syrian refugees but the Lebanese national curriculum was still taught to them. UNRWA facilitated schooling by integrating Palestinian Refugees from Syria (PRS) and Palestinian Refugees in Lebanon in classes based on their levels and abilities.

There has also been an increase in the number of Syrian coalition schools. These schools follow the Syrian national curriculum, as they did back in Syria but it includes criticisms of the Ba'ath Party and Assad regime. Syrian teachers and educators teach all subjects in the schools.

They deliver all their subjects including mathematics and science in Arabic and not in French or English like the Lebanese curriculum. The Libyan curriculum for Year 12 was offered through coalition schools and exams for the Baccalaureate were held in Turkey and transported to Libya for correction and accreditation. On the other hand, the formal NGO schools mostly personalised and modified the MoEHE curriculum, while the non-formal NGOs provided basic education; they lacked official certification with the focus being on retention rates. It was brought to the authors' attention that many NGO schools only offer educational programs in emergency situations and most of the time funding runs out half way through the academic year (Shuayb, Makkouk & Tuttunji, 2014).

Bullying and punishment

During the interviews that Nina conducted in some areas, there were indications of violence and bullying in schools. She heard stories about children being abused physically in Beirut and the north and the following statements were documented: "the teacher hit me with the ruler on my shoulder and hit my ear so I started bleeding"; "I hate going to school because Sir always slaps me when I don't know the answer"; another reported "if we get caught talking we get a beating with the tree branches".

These were statements made by young children between seven and twelve years of age. When Nina broached this topic with various school teachers and principals, many stated that this type of physical punishment should be stopped and also suggested that by involving the parents in the school and community these issues of abuse might come to an end. Mr Wael said the only way to stop this from happening was to have a law introduced that forbids such acts and it was something that the Lebanese government needed to proceed with. He also suggested that by having both Syrian and Lebanese families taking active roles in schools, such as sport, reading, recess supervision, etc., relationships between parents, teachers and school administration would be encouraged and strengthened.

Conclusion

As with the local school communities, the Lebanese government clearly recognises the need to actively support Syrian refugee children attending school. When they are supported by the United Nations agencies and other international aid organisations, the Syrian refugees benefit much more. The Lebanese government, however, is faced with huge challenges with the massive influx of refugees, and provision of public schooling is simply one of these many problems. With only a small percentage of these refugee children able to access and attend school, much remains to be done.

While accusations concerning mistreatment Syrian refugee children in schools are prevalent, these accusations exist in most countries – well-grounded by the authors' anecdotal accounts in Australian schools. These are problems easier solved in schools when compared to the broader community, given there are circumstances where students avoid school and turn to crime. Schools remain the best places to help the refugee children and their families to find a solution to these problems.

How then can perspectives of the State of the host country explain the pedagogy of the displaced? From the perspectives of the authorities, themes that emerged included: politics of documention, recognition, accredition and certification of refugee children's previous schooling; curricular challenges and addressing the language barrier; host state's provision of basic needs and other opportunities (employment and education); collaborative partnership between the host state, host communities, refugee communities and international aid organisations; recognition and support of non-formal schooling; addressing bullying and corporal punishment; and school-parents partnership and understanding for Syrian children refugees and Lebanese children.

Freire (1970) argued that education is a political process, and the host country/state and the international community is being called upon to support the refugee children defend the children's right to education and schooling in order to equip them to find the means to liberate themselves from poverty and lack of opportunities, to help them find solutions to conflict and struggle for social change and for a better future for themselves. This decision is indeed political and those in power have the authority and capacity to facilitate social change for the refugee children.

References

Addis, J. (2013, 2 April). Syria Q & A: Humanitarian crisis deepens. *World Vision Magazine.* Retrieved 16 February 2015, from <http://www.worldvisionmagazine.org/story/syria-qa-humanitarian-crisis-deepen>.

Centre for Lebanese Studies. (2014, 12 July). Press release: Challenges preventing Syrian refugee children from receiving an education tackled at Amman Conference. Retrieved 28 February 2015, from <http://lebanesestudies.com/press-release-challenges-preventing-syrian-refugee-children-from-receiving-an-education-tackled-at-amman-conference/>.

Freire, P. (1970). *Pedagody of the oppressed.* New York: Continuum.

International Labour Organisation. (2014). Assessment of the impact of Syrian refugees in Lebanon and their employment profile. *International Labour Organisation Regional Office for Arab States-Beirut.* Retrieved 26 January 2015, from <www.ilo.org/publns>.

Migration Policy Centre. (2014). Syrian refugees: A snapshot of the crisis-in the Middle East and Europe. Retrieved 15 December 2014, from <http://syrianrefugees.eu/?page_id=195>.

Prier, P. (2015, 19 January). Syrian refugees spell double trouble for Lebanese village. *Al-Araby Al-Jadeed English.* Retrieved 25 February 2015, from <http://www.alaraby.co.uk/english/features/233ffff9–5b6f-42fd-9580–89eb0d9e19ed?gclid=CM2Z1c3f9sMCFYSVvQodMF0A2A>.

Rainey, V. (2014, 19 November). In Lebanon, non-formal education programmes bring Syrian refugee children back to learning. *Children of Syria.* Retrieved 25 February 2015, from <http://childrenofsyria,info/2014/11/19in-lebanon-non-formal-education-programmes-bring-syrian-refugee-children-back-to-learning/>.

Shuayb, M., Makkouk, N. & Tuttunji, S. (2014). Widening access to quality education for Syrian refugees: The role of private and NGO sectors in Lebanon. Retrieved 13 October 2014, from <http://www.alnap.org/resource/19984>.

United Nations High Commissioner for Refugees (UNHCR). (2015a). Country operation profile: Lebanon. Retrieved 28 February 2015, from <http://www.unhcr.org/pages/49e486676.html>.
United Nations High Commissioner for Refugees (UNHCR). (2014b). Syrian refugee crisis- inter-agency regional update. Retrieved 24 January 2015, from <www.data.unhcr.org/syrianrefugees/regional.php>.
United Nations High Commissioner for Refugees (UNHCR). (2014c). Barriers to education for Syrian refugee children in Lebanon. Retrieved 10 April 2015, from <http://www.proasyl.de/fileadmin/proasyl/fm_redakteure/Newsletter_Anhaenge/207/reach_lbn_report_syriacrisis_outofschoolchildrenprofiling_nov2014.pdf>.
United Nations High Commissioner for Refugees (UNHCR). (2014d). Second shift schools offer hope to young Syrians. Retrieved 26 January 2015, from <www.unhcr.org/530b65326.html>.
World Vision. (2013). Syrian refugee crisis. Retrieved 27 February 2015, from <https://www.worldvision.com.au/Libraries/syria_appeal_card/Emergency-Syria-Situation-Report.pdf>.

GENERAL CONCLUSION

The Syrian civil war crisis, which has now been going on for over four years, has led to an extraordinarily huge number of refugees scattered throughout the Middle East. More than one million Syrian refugees with the majority being women and children, have arrived in Lebanon since 2011, seeking refuge from a bloody civil war that has taken over their home country. This large number of refugees trying to settle in a small place with a population of only four million people has impacted significantly on the country's economy and social cohesion. Lebanon itself had just been trying to recover from a few decades of civil war and the country's infrastructure is fragile.

Lebanon's public services are under pressure from having to help a large number of people, both locals and refugees. Similarly, education is suffering and schools lack the space and the ability to cater for all the Lebanese students as well as the refugees. As indicated by UNHCR (2014c), the number of refugee school children aged between 6 and 14 in Lebanon is 420,000. All of the children require education and have the right to it, but where schools can fit them all and how can they cater to all of their needs, will remain a challenge for the authorities. There are many problems that Nina discussed in previous chapters preventing access to education; they range from lack of space, financial limitations, transportation, language barriers and the curriculum, shortage of trained teachers and access to official documentation. These barriers are dealt with differently from one area to another. For example, in some areas, schools provide free transport to the children, while in others this facility is not available. Moreover, many refugees are not registered and therefore are not entitled to financial support and free education.

Despite teaching logistics such as double shifts that most schools have implemented to accommodate more students, the problem has not yet been solved. According to the statistics and reports from the UNHCR similar to the one mentioned above, it is evident that a large number of refugee children are not attending schools. What will happen when the extra students decide to enroll and start their schooling? The majority of teachers interviewed by Nina were keen to work extra few hours each school day and include the extra pupils in their classes, in order to make up for not having enough spaces in the classrooms for all students. However, the teachers are clearly under pressure and becoming very worn out.

Another set back for refugees preventing them from sending their children to school was the lack of transportation as a few interviewees intimated to Nina. It is a serious problem in that some children had to walk for a good 25 to 30 minutes before reaching their schools. This was a concern to a few who had several children but not all of them were going to school; some also had adults who needed constant care and could not be left while walking their children to school. A few parents mentioned the harsh weather conditions – especially winter because it can be extremely cold and snowy. The biggest fear for all parents was their children's safety while walking to school. They were worried about them being criticised, insulted, bullied and even physically abused.

An additional hurdle was the difference between the Lebanese and Syrian curricula. Having a second language implemented in the curriculum apart from Arabic and needing to master it, so that science, physics and maths lessons and official exams were achievable, created a considerable concern for most students on their arrival in Lebanon. According to people's comments when they were interviewed by Nina, the young generation of school children seem to be enjoying learning a second language and their parents are happy to hear them practise and sing. They are, however, worried about the lack of help they can provide for them if needed; students who are in the middle and senior school stages are struggling and feel left behind due to the language cordon.

A further challenge was that many refugees simply lacked official documentation to verify their children's schooling achievements. This created a number of issues between the schools and the Ministry of Education because some schools gave permission for the students to continue on with their studies regardless of the paper work, while the Ministry of Education insisted that each student wanting to sit for the official exam must provide – prior to registering for the examination – all the official documentation required. This generated heartaches and headaches in many parents who had no other option but to either send their children to sit official exams in Syria while they waited for their safe return. Or they had to risk the safety and life of a family member to go back to Syria and obtain such documentation.

One more dilemma that some refugees are facing is that of registration. As documented in previous chapters, some refugees mentioned to Nina that they crossed the Lebanese border illegally and now are too scared to register because they fear retaliation towards family members left in Syria. These people do not receive any benefits and don't have the right to work or get their children to attend school. They are basically stateless, but they "are alive, and not risking their loved one's life".

How do the perspectives of children, their parents, teachers and the community, and the host state inform the pedagody of the displaced?

The condition of social disadvantage that the Syrian refugee children and their families are experiencing is socially constructed, and the displaced had little to do with the conflict that is happening in their country. Those responsible for their condition of displacement made the political decision to engage in a war that did not only rob them of viable economic opportunities but also a homeland. The refugee children and their families now face limited or no economic opportunities in a foreign land that at the very least allowed them refuge. The host country and world community must take the side of the displaced and intervene in their social disadvantage, first and foremost, and fight on their side for social transformation. This may sound insurmountable but this is where education and schooling becomes vital to the liberation of the displaced, particulary the children, from the dehumanising compulsion to just survive. This is where the refugees encounter the politics of hospitality.

The pedagogy of the displaced refocuses the nature of the learner, their learning and teaching. The refugee learner inherited economic and social difficulties and experiences them first-hand. They are limited by the language of instruction of the host country, as well as the curricular expectations to achieve a certificate of education. With the knowledge that the children already possess, teaching has to proceed from how they make meaning of the world they are in. Teachers must understand how they learn and address the instances when they lose hope and self-deprecate, which may be signs of trauma. Teachers face a challenging task that requires much fortitude, perseverance and humility if they are to encourage the refugee children's resilience in learning. The pedagogy of the displaced also seeks out the concerted collaborative action of society – the refugee families, the schools, the communities, the host state, the international aid agencies and the rest of the world – in addressing the barriers to education and schooling of the refugee children. This means continued efforts to provide basic needs (food, shelter, clothing and sanitation), parental employment, capacity of public schools in the host communities, funding and incentives to non-formal schooling and volunteerism, school bus services, support services for counselling, mechanisms to address child labour and practicable arrangement for curricular concerns and accreditation issues. The pedagogy of the displaced attempts to address the barriers to education and schooling of the refugee children in order for them to learn, imagine and build a better future for themselves.

Reference

United Nations High Commissioner for Refugees (UNHCR). (2014c). Barriers to education for Syrian refugee children in Lebanon. Retrieved 10 April 2015, from <http://www.proasyl.de/fileadmin/proasyl/fm_redakteure/Newsletter _Anhaenge/207/reach_lbn_report_syriacrisis_outofschoolchildrenprofiling_nov2014.pdf>.

Appendix

The pedagogy of the displaced and its dimensions and how the dimensions inform it through the perspectives of the children, their parents/family, teachers, members of the community (host and refugee), the host country (the state) and the rest of the international community (other countries, the UN and its agencies and international aid and charitable institutions).

References

Abouawn, O. (2012). Syrian Arab Republic. In I. V. S. Mullis, M. O. Martin, C. A. Minnich, G. M. Stanco, A. Arora, V. A. S. Centurino & C. E. Castle (Eds.), *TIMSS 2011 Encyclopedia Education Policy and Curriculum in Mathematics and Science, Volume 2 : L–Z and Benchmarking Participants* (pp. 895–905). Boston: TIMSS & PIRLS International Study Center.

Abouchedid, K., Nasser, R. & Blommestein, J. (2002). The limitations of inter-group learning in confessional school systems: the case of Lebanon. *Arab Studies Quarterly*, Vol.24, no.4, pp.61–74.

Addis, J. (2013, 2 April). Syria Q & A: Humanitarian crisis deepens. *World Vision Magazine.* Retrieved 16 February 2015, from <http://www.worldvisionmagazine.org/story/syria-qa-humanitarian-crisis-deepen>.

Aljarida Alrasmiya of the Republic of Lebanon. (1977). *Laws and decrees concerningt he pre-university educational system*. Beirut: Sader Publications.

Amnesty International Australia. (2014, 1 July). Families torn apart as Palestinian refugees from Syria denied entry to Lebanon. Retrieved 19 February 2015, from <http://www.amnesty.org.au/news/comments/34938/>.

American Near East Refugee Aid (ANERA). (2014). Stories: Lebanon. Retrieved 12 January 2015, from <http://www.anera.org/locations/lebanon/>.

Barnett, L. (2002). *Global governance the evolution of the international regime*. New York: Oxford University Press.

Batha, E. (2013). Child marriage on rise among Syrian refugees-aid groups. *Thomson Reuters Foundation.* Retrieved 24 July 2014, from <http://www.trust.org/item/?map=child-marriage-on-rise-among-syrian-refugees-aid-groups/>.

Brett, R. & McCallin, M. (1996). *Children: The invisible soldiers*. Stockholm: Sewdish Save the Children.

Bridging Refugee Youth and Children's Services. (2006). *Educational handbook for refugee parents*. New York: International Rescue Committee.

Brown, G. (2014, 24 January). A brilliant scheme for making sure Syria's child refugees get and education. *The Guardian*. Retrieved 15 January 2015, from <http://www.theguardian.com/commentisfree/2014/jan/24/syria-child-refugees-school-education/>.

Bulley, D. (2014). Inside the tent: Community and government in refugee camps *Security Dialogue*.

Centre for Lebanese Studies. (2014, 12 July). Press release: Challenges preventing Syrian refugee children from receiving an education tackled at Amman Conference. Retrieved 28 February 2015, from <http://lebanesestudies.com/press-release-challenges-preventing-syrian-refugee-children-from-receiving-an-education-tackled-at-amman-conference/>.

Cervan, D. (2011). Religion in education and conflict: Lebanon and Northern Ireland compared. Retrieved 21 January 2014, from <https://www.ruor.uottawa.ca/bitstream/10393/20006/1/Cervan_Daniel_2011_thesis.pdf>.

Cochran, J. (2014). The education of Syrian refugee children. Retrieved 11 January 2015, from <http://www.mei.edu/content/at/education-syrian-refugee-children>.

Corbin, J. & Strauss, A. (1990). Grounded theory research: Procedures, canons, and evaluative criteria. *Qualitative Sociology, 13*(1), 3–21. doi: 10.1007/BF00988593.

Craissati, D. (2015). *Curriculum, accreditation and certification for Syrian children in Syria, Turkey, Lebanon, Jordan, Iraq and Egypt*. Amman: UNICEF MENA Regional Office.

Daou, R. (2014). Tent school offers hope to Syrian child refugees. *Yahoo News*. Retrieved 12 January 2015, from <http://news.yahoo.com/tent-school-offers-hope-syrian-child-refugees-041341979.html>.

Derrida, J. (2000) "Hospitality", *Angelaki: Journal of the Theoretical Humanities*, Vol. 5, no. 3, pp. 3–18.

Dingle, S. (2014). Epidemic of child marriage' for Syrian girl refugees, aid agency warns. *ABC The World Today*. Retrieved 24 July 2014, from <http://www.abc.net.au/worldtoday/content/2014/s4048084.htm>.

Drumm, R. D., Pittman, S. W. & Perry, S. (2004). Social work interventions in refugee camps. *Journal of Social Service Research, 30*(2), 67–92. doi: 10.1300/J079v30n02_05.

European Neighbourhood and Partnership instrument. (2007). *Lebanese Republic: Country Strategy and National Indicative Program.* Belguim: European External Action Service.

Fazel, M. & Stein, A. (2002). The mental health of refugee children. *Archives of Diseases in Childhood, 87*(5), 366–370.

Freire, P. (1970). *Pedagody of the oppressed.* New York: Continuum.

Ghosn, N. (2013). Lebanon's burden: The crushing consequences of Syria's refugee crisis. *Women's International League for Peace and Freedom.* Retrieved 20 December 2014, from <www.wilpfinternational.org/Lebanons-burden-the-crushing-consequences-of-syrias-refugees--crisis/org.com>.

Ghusayni, R., Akkary, R.K. & Akar, B. (2012). *Learning and teaching history: Lessons from and for Lebanon.* Beirut: Lebanese Association for Educational Studies.

Glaser, B. G. (2001). *The grounded theory perspective: Conceptualization contrasted with description.* Mill Valley, CA: Sociology Press.

Glaser, B. G. & Strauss, A. L. (1967). *The Discovery of Grounded Theory: Strategies for Qualitative Research.* London; New Brunswick: Aldine Transaction.

Gottfredson, D. C., Cook, P. J. & Na, C. (2011). School-based crime prevention. In B. C. Welsh & D. P. Farrington (Eds.), *The Oxford Handbook on Crime Prevention.* New York: Oxford University Press.

Grant, H. & Harper, L. (2013, 29 November). Syrian refugee children face catastrophic life in exile, UN says. *The Guardian.* Retrieved 24 August 2014, from <http://www.theguardian.com/global-development/2013/nov/29/syrian-refugee-children-catastrophe-exile-un>.

Hajjar, G. (2002). *Aspects of Christian -Muslim relations in contemporary Lebanon.* Lebanon: Notre Dame University.

Hamdan, H. (2013). Education in Lebanon - War Child Holland. Retrieved 24 January 2015, from <www.warchildholland.org>.

Harrison, K. (2011). Between politics and identity: The history and future of education in Lebanon. Retrieved 12 January 2015, from <www.tuftsgloballeadership.or/files/between_politics_identity.pdf>.

International Labour Organisation. (2014). Assessment of the impact of Syrian refugees in Lebanon and their employment profile. *International Labour Organisation Regional Office for Arab States-Beirut.* Retrieved 26 January 2015, from <www.ilo.org/publns>.

Kangarlou, T. (2015, 20 March). Lebanon schools struggle to integrate Syrian children. Retrieved 14 July 2015, from <http://www.almonitor.com/pulse/originals/2015/03/lebanoneducationcrisissyriarefugees childrenschools.html#>.

Lustig, S. L., Kia-Keating, M., Knight, W., Geltman, P., Ellis, H., Kinzie, J. D., Saxe, G. N. (2004). Review of child and adolescent refugee mental health. *Child and Adolescent Psychiatry, 43*(1), 24–36.

Lynch, S. & Faek, R. (2014, 15 September). As the school year starts, many refugees are shut out. Retrieved 22 January 2015, from <http://www.al-fanarmedia.org/2014/09/school-year-starts-many-refugees-shut/>.

Maadad, N. (2013). Lebanon: Post civil war implications for schools. In S. R. P. Clarke & T. A. O'Donoghue (Eds.), *School-level leadership in post- conflict societies* (pp. 127–144). Oxon; New York: Taylor & Francis.

Matthiesen, T. (2014). Key issues in religion and world affairs: Sectarianism in the Middle East. Retrieved 26 June 2015, from <http://www.bu.edu/cura/files/2013/10/Matthiesen.pdf>.

McCarthy, F. E. & Vickers, M. H. (2012). *Refugee and immigrant students: Achieving equity in education.* Charlotte, NC: Information Age Publishing.

Meikle, J. (2013, 4 June). Syrian disease outbreaks "inevitable", warns WHO. *The Guardian.* Retrieved 12 January 2015, from <http://www.theguardian.com/world/2013/jun/04/syrian-disease-outbreaks-inevit able-who>.

Migration Policy Centre. (2014). Syrian refugees: A snapshot of the crisis-in the Middle East and Europe. Retrieved 15 December 2014, from <http://syrianrefugees.eu/?page_id=195>.

Mikdadi, L. (1983). *Surviving the siege of Beirut: A personal account.* London: Onyx Press.

Millbank, A. (2000). *The problem with the 1951 Refugee Convention.* Canberra: Commonwealth of Australia Retrieved from <http://www.

aph.gov.au/About_Parliament/Parliamentary_Departments/Parliamentary_Library/pubs/rp/rp0001/01RP05>.

Miller, P. (1986). *Long division*. Adelaide: Wakefield Press.

Mills, C. W. (1963). *Power, politics and people*. New York: Galaxy.

Ministry of Education and Higher Education of Lebanon. (2012). Retrieved 12 January 2015, from <http://www.crdp.rof/CRDP/Arabic/ar-statistics/STAT>.

Ministry of Education and Higher Education of Lebanon. (2005). Retrieved 12 January 2015, from <http://www.crdp.rof/CRDP/Arabic/ar-statistics/STAT>.

Morrison, A., and K. O'Gorman (2008) "Hospitality Studies and Hospitality Management: A Symbiotic Relationship", *International Journal of Hospitality Management*, Vol. 27, pp. 214–221.

Mulford, B., Kendall, D., Ewington, J., Edmunds, B., Kendall, L. & Silins, H. (2008.). Successful principalship of high-performance schools in high-poverty communities. *Journal of Educational Administration, 46*(4), 461–480.

Mwancha, D. (2014). Former Somali refugees raise funds in Canada to build pre-school in Dadaab. Retrieved 24 July 2014, from <http://www.unrefugees.org.au/news-and-media/news-headlines/kenya-former-somali-refugees-raise-funds-in-canada-to-build-pre-school-in-dadaab>.

News.com.au. (2015, 27 March). Ex prime minister Malcolm Fraser farewelled in state funeral. Retrieved 29 March 2015, from <http://www.news.com.au/national/ex-prime-minister-malcolm-fraser-farewelled-in-state-funeral/story-fncynjr2–1227280853514>.

One Hope and Near East Initiative. (2013). Children in crisis. Retrieved 10 February 2015, from <http://onehope.net/wp-content/uploads/2014/04/Children-in-Crisis.pdf>.

Perini, M. (2013). Lebanon: School of Life in Marj El Khokh Camp, the experience of AVSI, the Italian NGO. Retrieved 15 August 2014, from <http://www.oasiscenter.eu/lebanon-schoollifeinmarjelkhokhcamp.html>.

Perumal, J. C. (2013). Pedagogy of refuge: education in a time of dispossession. *Race Ethnicity and Education, 16*(5), 673–695.

Porter, M. & Haslam, N. (2005). Predisplacement and postdisplacement factors associated with mental health of refugees and internally displaced persons. *The Journal of the American Medical Association, 294*(5), 602–612.

Powell, A. (2014, 5 February). Perilous plight for Syrian refugees in Lebanon, child exploitation, illness among concerns cited by researchers. *Harvard Gazette.* Retrieved 16 December 2014, from <http://news.harvard.edu/gazette/story/2014/02/plight-of-syrian-refugees-in-lebanon-becoming-desperate/>.

Prier, P. (2015, 19 January). Syrian refugees spell double trouble for Lebanese village. *Al-Araby Al-Jadeed English.* Retrieved 25 February 2015, from <http://www.alaraby.co.uk/english/features/233ffff9–5b6f-42fd-9580–89eb0d9e19ed?gclid=CM2Z1c3f9sMCFYSVvQodMF0A2A>.

Pritchett, L., Banerji, R. & Kenny, C. (2013). Schooling is not education! Using assessment to change the politics of non-learning. *A Report of the Center for Global Development Study Group on Measuring Learning Outcomes.* Retrieved 24 August 2014, from <http://www.cgdev.org/sites/default/files/schooling-is-not-learning-WEB.pdf>.

Rainey, V. (2014, 19 November). In Lebanon, non-formal education programmes bring Syrian refugee children back to learning. *Children of Syria.* Retrieved 25 February 2015, from <http://childrenofsyria,info/2014/11/19in-lebanon-non-formal-education-programmes-bring-syrian-refugee-children-back-to-learning/>.

Reynaert, D., Bouverne-de-Bie, M. & Vandevelde, S. (2009). A review of children's rights literature since the adoption of the United Nations Convention on the Rights of the Child. *Childhood, 16*(4), 518–534. doi: 10.1177/0907568209344270

Rosenthal, M. (2014). Lebanon aid groups scramble to build schools for Syrian refugee children. *The Huffington Post.* Retrieved 12 March 2014, from <http://www.huffingtonpost.com/2014/02/26/syrian-refugees-schools_n_4855751.html>.

SABER Country Report. (2010). Lebanon teachers. *World Bank.* Retrieved 29 January 2015, from <http://www.wbgfiles.worldbank.org>.

Save the Children. (2015). Small hands, heavy burden: How the Syria conflict is driving more children into the workforce. London: Save the Children; UNICEF.

Save the Children. (2014). Tens of thousands of Syrian child refugees out of school, warns Save the Children. Retrieved 3 January 2015, from

<http://www.scaemergency.org.au/tens-of-thousands-syrian-child-refugees-out-of-school>.
Simmons, A. (1985). *Immigration and Canada: Global and transnational perspectives*. Toronto, Ontario: Canadian Scholar's Press, Inc.
Shaheen, K. (2014a, 27 October). Schooling for Syrian refugee children gets inventive. *The Daily Star.* Retrieved 10 January 2015, from <www.dailystar.com.lb>.
Shaheen, K. (2014b, 18 September). Four out of five Syrian children in Lebanon lack schooling. Retrieved 22 November 2014, from <http://www.dailystar.com.lb/News/Lebanon-News/2014/Sep-18/271039-four-out-of-five-syrian-children-in-lebanon-lack-schooling.ashx>.
Shaheen, K. (2014c, 16 February). Syrian children forced to work on streets of Beirut face severe exploitation. *The Guardian.* Retrieved 20 February 2015, from <http://www.theguardian.com/world/2015/feb/16/syrian-children-forced-to-work-on-streets-of-beirut-face-severe-exploitation>.
Shuayb, M. (2014). A lost generation? Education opportunities for Syrian children in Lebanon. Retrieved 12 September 2014, from <http://www.rsc.ox.ac.uk/events/a-lost-generation-education-opportuni ties-for-syrian-refugee-children-in-lebanon>.
Shuayb, M., Makkouk, N. & Tuttunji, S. (2014). Widening access to quality education for Syrian refugees: The role of private and NGO sectors in Lebanon. Retrieved 13 October 2014, from <http://www.alnap.org/resource/19984>.
Sidhu, R. & Taylor, S. (2012), "Supporting Refugee Students in Schools: what constitutes inclusive education?" *International Journal of Inclusive Education*, vol. 16, no. 1, pp. 39–56.
Spencer, R. (2015, 1 April). Surrendering to the camera, a four-year-old Syrian girl. *Daily Telegraph.* Retrieved 2 April 2015, from <http://www.telegraph.co.uk/news/worldnews/middleeast/syria/11508306/Surrendering-to-the-camera-a-four-year-old-Syrian-girl.html>.
Taylor, J. (2004). Refugees and social exclusion: What the literature says. *Migration Action, 26*(2), 16–31.
The European Graduate School. (2012). Biography: Jean-Luc Nancy. Retrieved 3 July 2015, from <http://www.egs.edu/faculty/jean-luc-nancy/biography/>.

Thibos, C. (2014). One million Syrians in Lebanon: A milestone quickly passed. Retrieved 5 November 2014, from <http://www.migrationpolicycentre.eu/>.

Thomas, C. M., Calvo, R. & Loughry, M. (2015). Refugee health and wellbeing: Differences between urban and camp-based environments in Sub-Saharan Africa. Retrieved from Journal of Refugee Studies website: <http://jrs.oxfordjournals.org/content/early/2015/04/15/jrs.fev003.short?rss=1,doi:10.1093/jrs/fev003>.

Thornberg, R. (2012). Informed grounded theory. *Scandinavian Journal of Educational Research, 56*(3), 243–259. doi: 10.1080/00313831.2011.581686

Toronto, J. & Eissa, M. (2007). Egypt: Promoting tolerance, defending against Islamism. In E. Abdellah & G. Starrett (Eds.), *Teaching Islam* (pp. 27–51). London: Lynne Reinner Publishers.

United Nations Educational, Scientific & Cultural Organization (UNESCO). (2013). Syrian refugees education: Country profile. Retrieved 7 July 2015, from <http://www.unesco.org/new/fileadmin/MULTIMEDIA/FIELD/Beirut/images/Lebanon_Country_Profile.pdf>.

United Nations Educational, Scientific & Cultural Organization (UNESCO). (2008). Institute for statistics database. Retrieved 12 January 2015, from <www.uis.unesco.org>.

United Nations High Commissioner for Refugees (UNHCR). (2015a). Country operation profile - Lebanon. Retrieved 28 February 2015, from <http://www.unhcr.org/pages/49e486676.html>.

United Nations High Commissioner for Refugees (UNHCR). (2015b). The 1951 Refugee Convention,. Retrieved 3 July 2015, from <http://www.unhcr.org/pages/49da0e466.html>.

United Nations High Commissioner for Refugees (UNHCR). (2014a). 2014 Syria regional resopnse plan: Education. *Vulnerability Assessment for Syrian Refugees (VASyR), WFP, UNHCR, UNICEF.* Retrieved 14 July 2015, from <http://www.unhcr.org/syriarrp6/midyear/index.html>.

United Nations High Commissioner for Refugees (UNHCR). (2014b). Syrian refugee crisis- inter-agency regional update. Retrieved 24 January 2015, from <www.data.unhcr.org/syrianrefugees/regional.php>.

United Nations High Commissioner for Refugees (UNHCR). (2014c). Barriers to education for Syrian refugee children in Lebanon. Retrieved 10 April 2015, from <http://www.proasyl.de/fileadmin/proasyl/fm_redakteure/Newsletter _Anhaenge/207/reach_lbn_report_syriacrisis_outofschoolchildrenprofiling_nov2014.pdf>.

United Nations High Commissioner for Refugees (UNHCR). (2013a). The challenge of education: The future of Syria refugee children in crisis. Retrieved 20 September 2014, from <http://www.unhcr.org/syria/the-challenge-of-education>.

United Nations High Commissioner for Refugees (UNHCR). (2013b). Syria regional response plan. Geneva: UNHCR.

United Nations High Commissioner for Refugees (UNHCR). (2013c). The challenge of education: The future of Syria refugee children in crisis. Retrieved 20 September 2014, from <http://www.unhcr.org/syria/the-challenge-of-education>.

United Nations High Commissioner for Refugees (UNHCR). (2009). UNHCR Policy on refugee protection and solution in urban areas. Retrieved 26 June 2015, from <http://www.unhcr.org/4ab356ab6.pdf>.

United Nations High Commissioner for Refugees (UNHCR). (2001). Learning for a future: Refugee education in developing countries. Retrieved 24 July 2014, from <http://www.unhcr.org/4a1d5ba36.html>.

United Nations Human Rights Council. (2006). Resolution adopted by the General Assembly on 15 March 2006. Retrieved 12 January 2015, from <http://www.daccess-dds-ny.un.org>.

United Nations International Children's Emergency Fund (UNICEF). (2015). Lebanon street-based children report. *#ChildrenofSyria*. Retrieved 15 July 2015, from <http://childrenofsyria.info/2015/02/16/lebanon-street-based-children-report-2015–2/>.

United Nations International Children's Emergency Fund (UNICEF) (2013), *Syrian refugees and other affected populations in Iraq, Jordan, Lebanon, Turkey and Egypt*. New York: UNICEF Humanitarian Action for Children.

United Nations International Children's Emergency Fund (UNICEF). (2007). The humanitarian action report. Retrieved 12 January 2015, from <www.unicef.org/har07/index.html>.

United Nations International Children's Emergency Fund (UNICEF). (2004). The state of the world's children. Retrieved 12 January 2015, from <www.unicef.org/sowc04>.

United Nations International Children's Emergency Fund (UNICEF). (1996). Girls' education: A lifeline to development. *The State of the World's Children*. Retrieved 12 March 2015, from <http://www.unicef.org/sowc96/ngirls.htm>.

Unite for Sight. (2015). Module 4: Children and education in refugee camps. Retrieved 22 August 2015, from <http://www.uniteforsight.org/refugee-health/module4>.

Wakim, J. (2013, 18 July). What can Lebanon teach Australia about refugees? *The Drum*. Retrieved 12 March 2015, from <http://mobile.abc.net.au/news/2013–07-18/wakim---a-global-perspective-on-refugees/4828412>.

War Child Holland. (2016). Strengthening education for vulnerable Syrian and Lebanese children in Northern Lebanon. *War Child*. Retrieved 20 September 2014, from <http://www.warchildholland.org/project/strengthening-education-vulnerable-syrian-and-lebanese-children-northern-lebanon>.

Watkins, K. (2014). It is time for a "New Deal" on education for Syrian refugee children. *The Huffington Post*. Retrieved 12 January 2015, from <http://www.huffingtonpost.com/>.

Whyte, S. & Ting, I. (2014, 21 June). As world refugee numbers hit 50 million, Australia goes backwards. *Sydney Morning Herald*. Retrieved 24 July, 2014, from <http://www.smh.com.au/national/as-world-refugee-numbers-hit-50-million-australia-goes-backwards-20140620–3ajqj.html>.

Wood, J. (2015, 2 March). Syrian refugees struggle to bury dead as life in Lebanon becomes permanent. *Foreign Correspondent*. Retrieved 10 March 2015, from <http://www.bbc.com/news/world-middle-east-31001100>.

Wood, P. (2015, 8 January). Winter ordeal for Syrian refugees in makeshift camps. *BBC News Middle East*. Retrieved 12 January 2015, from <http://www.bbc.com/news/world-middle-east-30725558>.

World Vision. (2013). Syrian refugee crisis. Retrieved 27 February 2015, from <https://www.worldvision.com.au/Libraries/syria_appeal_card/Emergency-Syria-Situation-Report.pdf>.

World Vision. (2015, 12 May). FAQs: Syria's war, children, and the refugee crisis. Retrieved 8 August 2015, from <http://www.worldvision.org/news-stories-videos/faqs-war-syria-children-and-refugee-crisis>.

Xie, Y. & Greenman, E. (2011). The social context of assimilation: testing implications of segmented assimilation theory. *Social Science Research, 40*(3), 965–984.

Yacoubian, M. (2014). Renewed conflict in Lebanon. *Council on Foreign Relations*. Retrieved 7 July 2015, from <http://www.cfr.org/lebanon/renewed-conflict-lebanon/p33083>.

Zaatari, M. (2013, 14 September). Sidon schools overwhelmed by number of refugees. *The Daily Star Lebanon*. Retrieved 24 January 2015, from <http://www.dailystar.com.lb/News/Lebanon-News/2013/Sep-14/231234-sidon-schools-overwhelmed-by-number-of-refugees.ashx>.